Community and the Politics of Place

Community and the Politics of Place

by Daniel Kemmis

University of Oklahoma Press : Norman and London

For Deva, John, Abe & Sam
Wee must delight in eache other . . .

Library of Congress Cataloging-in-Publication Data

Kemmis, Daniel, 1945–
    Community and the politics of place / by Daniel Kemmis.
        p.   cm.
    Includes bibliographical references.
    ISBN 0-8061-2227-7 (alk. paper)
    1. Political culture—West (U.S.)—History.   2. Man—Influence of envi-
ronment—West (U.S.)—History.   3. Geographical perception.   4. West
(U.S.)—Politics and government.   5. West (U.S.)—Economic policy.
I. Title.
JK2687.K46   1990
306.2'0978—dc20   89-25023
                                                                                      CIP

The paper in this book meets the guidelines for permanence and durability of the Committee on Production Guidelines for Book Longevity of the Council on Library Resources, Inc.ⓧ

The United States shall guarantee to every State in the Union a Republican Form of Government. [United States Constitution, Article IV, Section 4]

   . . . Republican? . . .

In an extensive republic the public good is sacrificed to a thousand private views; it is subordinate to exceptions, and depends on accidents. In a small one, the interest of the public is more obvious, better understood, and more within the reach of every citizen. [Montesquieu]

   . . . Within reach? . . .

Keeping citizens apart has become the first maxim of modern politics. [Rousseau]

   . . . Why keep them apart? . . .

Extend the sphere, and you take in a greater variety of parties and interests; you make it less probable that a majority of the whole will have a common motive to invade the rights of other citizens; or if such a common motive exists, it will be more difficult for all who feel it to discover their own strengths and to act in unison with each other. [James Madison, *The Federalist Papers*, No. 51 (1788)]

   . . . But what about the republic? . . .

This reliance [upon the people] cannot deceive us, as long as we remain virtuous, and I think we shall be so, as long as agriculture is our principal object, which will be the case, while there remains vacant lands in any part of America. [Letter from Thomas Jefferson to James Madison, December 20, 1787]

   . . . Vacant lands? . . .

And now, four centuries from the discovery of America, at the end of a hundred years of life under the Constitution, the frontier has gone, and with its going has closed the first period of American history. [Frederick Jackson Turner, *The Significance of the Frontier in American History* (1893)]

   . . . No new places? . . .

In politics "the place" is a mental habitat, an intellectual and moral landscape. To know clearly, perhaps even for the first time, the defective philosophic premises of our nation should not mean loving the nation less. . . . Because a nation is, to some extent, a state of mind, knowing a nation in a new way makes the nation into a new place. [George Will, *Statecraft as Soulcraft* (1983)]

Anniversaries
1987–1992

1492: Europe discovers a new frontier
  1787: United States Constitution drafted
    1788: Constitution ratified
      1789: Congress proposes Bill of Rights
        1791: Bill of Rights ratified by states
          1889: Montana, North and South Dakota admitted to the Union
           1890: Idaho and Wyoming admitted to the Union; Census Bureau declares the frontier closed

Contents

Acknowledgments

This book was written under a grant from the William and Flora Hewlett Foundation, which enabled the Northern Lights Research and Education Institute to give me a home and a terminal and endless intellectual stimulation. Everyone at Northern Lights has contributed ideas or useful criticism and constant support of every kind for my work. The better half of this book belongs to Carol Abrams and Bill Clarke, Deborah Clow and Maeta Kaplan, Richard Opper and Don Snow.

The Matthew Hansen Wilderness Studies Endowment assisted with research into the relationship of open land to public life.

I am especially grateful to Robert Barrett at the Hewlett Foundation for his interest in my work and his suggestions about worthwhile reading. Chris Carlson at the Charles F. Kettering Foundation has also guided me to good books, and she above all has introduced me to the civic conversation by enabling me to meet some of its best practitioners. Talks with Benjamin Barber, Jeff Bercuvitz, Harry Boyte, Elizabeth Minnich, and William Sullivan have deepened substantially my appreciation for both the difficulties and the possibilities of public life.

Many people have read and commented upon the manuscript, and I have never failed to profit from their advice. Ron Perrin and Richard Walton were especially helpful.

My students have convinced me that it is worth saying, even if you haven't quite got it right yet. They have helped me appreciate the role of hope in public life.

Albert Borgmann introduced me to the meaning of practice, and he has been willing to struggle with me endlessly over the relationship of practices to politics. He also taught me why friendship and philosophy belong together.

Jeanne Kemmis has shown me the meaning of householding, at home and in the world. That turned out to be the heart of the matter.

Community and the Politics of Place

CHAPTER ONE

Pre-Amble

(An Introductory Stroll)

At first glance, the preambles to the constitutions of Montana and of the United States seem very similar. They both begin with the words "We the people," and they both end with those people declaring their intention to "ordain and establish" the constitution in question. But in between those clauses there is a noteworthy difference.

The Preamble to the United States Constitution begins, "We the People of the United States, in order to form a more perfect union . . . ," and then proceeds to list the other compelling reasons for establishing this new government. The language is concise, eloquent, and utterly instrumental. Certain ends of government having been identified, the Constitution is to be the instrument for attaining them—period.

Montana's preamble contains many of the same elements. It begins, as the federal preamble does, by identifying who is speaking; it ends by ordaining its constitution; and in between it makes it clear that these people are ordaining this government in order to achieve certain specified ends. But before getting down to the instrumental nitty gritty, the people of Montana had something else to say: "We the people of Montana, *grateful to God for the quiet beauty of our state,*

the grandeur of its mountains, the vastness of its rolling plains, and desiring
to secure to ourselves and our posterity the blessings of liberty for
this and future generations do ordain and establish this constitution"
[emphasis added].

Why did the authors of this constitution pause to express their
gratitude for the Montana landscape? It would be possible to argue
that they were simply being long-winded in a document which
should be lean and concise to a fault. But it can also be argued
that those Montanans said not a word more than they had to say,
but that they had to say more than their federal counterparts
because they were expressing a different attitude toward self-
government than were the Founding Fathers. They were saying that
the way they felt about the place they inhabited was an important
part of what they meant when they said "We the people." They had
not come to know each other as "we" simply "in order to"; they
knew each other as "we" in relation to that place. So, in constituting
themselves as a people, they could not pretend to do it in purely
instrumental terms.

A constitution is more than a legal document. It is the single most
expressive act by which separate, individual people *constitute* themselves as *a people*. A people so constituted is, in turn, the only genuine
source of meaning for the word *public*, which, in Latin, meant "of
the people." It does not simply mean "of people." People in their
separated individuality never become public. They only do that by a
deliberate act of constituting themselves as "the people." The Montana and United States preambles are worth studying because they
hint at a fundamental difference in the way "we" identify and
constitute ourselves as "the people"—a difference, in other words,
in our understanding of our public selves.

It is doubtful if any society has ever used the word *public* as
incessantly as we now do. We have public hearings to help us shape
public policy about issues like public lands, public education, public
welfare, and public health. In all of these areas, special groups are
formed to pursue the public interest, while politicians base their
public policy decisions increasingly upon the results of public opin-

ion polls. It would be strange indeed to discover that we Americans, who use the word *public* in more contexts than ever before, had lost almost all sense of what that word might actually mean. Because we use the word so much, we not unnaturally assume that it must mean something. But steadily falling voter turnout, polls which show a progressive loss of trust in all government institutions, and other indicators of a waning confidence in our ability to govern ourselves should tell us that the public dimension of our lives is losing its vitality.

As the word *public* has become both more ubiquitous and less meaningful, the old eighteenth century word *republican* has simply faded from use. Until very recently, that word, in anything but its capitalized, partisan form, had all but disappeared from the American political lexicon. But now a remarkable number of people are again using the word *republican* the way people like Thomas Jefferson once used it. The next chapter will examine Jefferson's understanding of republicanism, and we will see there how Jefferson feared that public life would be endangered anytime that it was removed from its re*public*an context. Before turning to Jefferson's specific concerns, it may be worthwhile to spend a moment with the word itself. The Latin phrase was *res publica*—the "public thing." Now there, at first glance, is a genuinely vacuous phrase. If the word *public* has lost meaning, we seem to add precious little content by referring to the "public thing." So how could the concept of a "republic" provide a meaningful context for the word *public*? Hannah Arendt offers this perspective on the relationship of the public and the *res*:

> To live together in the world means essentially that a world of things is between those who have it in common, as a table is located between those who sit around it; the world, like every in-between, relates and separates men at the same time.
>
> The public realm, as the common world, gathers us together and yet prevents our falling over each other, so to speak. What makes mass society so difficult to bear is not the number of people involved, or at

least not primarily, but the fact that the world between them has lost its power to gather them together, to relate and to separate them. The weirdness of this situation resembles a spiritualistic seance where a number of people gathered around a table might suddenly, through some magic trick, see the table vanish from their midst, so that two persons sitting opposite each other were no longer separated but also would be entirely unrelated by anything tangible.[1]

This vanishing table is the thing—the *res*—which would make a "public" possible. It is just this which is suggested by the Montana preamble, where the eminently tangible mountains and plains of the state play precisely the role of gathering people together by simultaneously relating and separating them. The U.S. preamble (and indeed most of what we now call "public" life) attempts to dispense altogether with that gathering and separating "thing." We have severed the public from its republican context. In the process, we have made any real public life all but impossible. Our question, then, is what happened to the public thing: How did the table vanish? Part of the answer lies in what happened to our understanding of public life at certain key periods in our political history. The next two chapters will explore some of that history. But the demise of public life has to be understood in terms of space (or place) as well as time. Putting it more positively, public life can only be reclaimed by understanding, and then practicing, its connection to real, identifiable places. This is not a particularly easy way for most of us to think about public issues. Thinking of politics in historical terms is second nature, but we tend to be more dubious about the proposition that political culture may be shaped by its place, as well as by its time.

Most of the current literature on the revival of "civic republicanism" is highly abstract, addressing those elements of a renewed public philosophy which would be appropriate in any location. This is a valuable body of work, and my own indebtedness to it is apparent throughout this book. But this republican renaissance has not yet addressed itself to the prevailing placelessness of our political culture. Public life as we all too often experience it now is very much like a Big Mac—it can be replicated, in exactly the same form, anywhere. And just as our acceptance of placeless "food," consumed under placeless yellow "landmarks," weakens both our sense of food and of place, so too does the general placelessness of our political thought weaken both our sense of politics and of place. This weakening is foreshadowed by the demise of the word *republic*, but it is also implicit in the infrequency with which we use the term *political culture*. No real culture—whether we speak of food or of politics or of anything else—can exist in abstraction from place. Yet that abstraction is one of the hallmarks of our time. Wendell Berry describes our situation, in terms which can and should be applied to our understanding of public life:

> We have given up the understanding—dropped it out of our language and so out of our thought—that we and our country create one another, depend on one another, are literally part of one another; that our land passes in and out of our bodies just as our bodies pass in and out of our land; that as we and our land are part of one another, so all who are living as neighbors here, human and plant and animal, are part of one another, and so cannot possibly flourish alone; that, therefore, our culture must be our response to our place, our culture and our place are images of each other and inseparable from each other, and so neither can be better than the other.[2]

The preamble to Montana's constitution, with its expression of gratitude for Montana's landscape, reflects an understanding however faint that the political culture of a place is not something apart from the place itself. By exactly the same token, the strengthening of political culture, the reclaiming of a vital and effective sense of what it is to be public, must take place and must be studied in the context of very specific places and of the people who struggle to live well in such places. This book is one effort to do that. What follows here may be seen as a pattern of concentric circles, with the focus sharpening as the scope of attention becomes more local. Some of the discussion will be applicable on a global scale. More of it will be restricted to national relevance. There will be a substantial emphasis on the way the revival of public life is happening or could happen in one particular region of the country—the region which joined the nation just as the old American frontier ceased to exist. Within that region, I will refer more often to the state of my own birth and work than any other, and I will tend to draw local examples of community building from my own home community in western Montana. This method of focusing is not in any sense meant to imply that this particular locality, or this state or this region, or even this nation, has a unique role to play in the revitalization of civic culture. The point is that every place has a unique contribution to make to that work, but that no place can play that role until we become much more sharply aware of how our places shape our politics.

The role of place in American public life was an important sub-theme of the debates over the ratification of the U.S. Constitution—and the way that issue was resolved then has influenced our public life ever since. We need, then, to make a brief stop in Philadelphia in the summer of 1787.

Notes

1. Hannah Arendt, *The Human Condition*, pp. 52–53. While Arendt's presentation of the "thingness" of the *res publica* is central to my own understanding of the conditions of public life, it should be noted that Arendt would not agree at all with my application of the concept of the *res* to mountains and rivers. Arendt insisted that public things were necessarily the work of human hands. This is not the place to argue the point, but I do want to clear Arendt of any responsibility for a use of the concept of the *res publica* with which she would not agree.

2. Wendell Berry, *The Unsettling of America*, p. 22.

Keeping Citizens Apart

"I'd rather be in Philadelphia." There was only one place from which W. C. Fields could even imagine saying such a thing, so he asked that those words be inscribed on his gravestone. By contrast, in the summer of 1787, Thomas Jefferson would have taken Fields' epitaph as his own heartfelt motto. Never mind that Jefferson found himself in one of the world's most elegant settings, the palace of Versailles, where he was serving as American ambassador to France. Never mind that Philadelphia was hot, muggy, and muddy enough to have reconfirmed W. C. Fields in his most vituperative opinions of the City of Brotherly Love. For Jefferson, what mattered was that a new government was being formed in Philadelphia, and he was not there to help. So he chafed at his post, waited impatiently for every bit of news about what the delegates were concocting, and wrote a steady stream of letters analyzing the proposed charter.

When the document was completed in September, Jefferson found himself deeply ambivalent about it. "How do you like our new constitution?" he wrote to John Adams. "I confess there are things in it which stagger all my dispositions to subscribe to what such an assembly has proposed."[1] The lack of a bill of rights was simply intolerable to Jefferson. Limitless terms of office for the presidency struck him as an open invitation to monarchy. He could not see how the House of Representatives could function as an effective legislative assembly. But behind all these worries was a deeper one.

Jefferson knew that many of the delegates had gone to Philadelphia in the spring of 1787 deeply shaken by the insurrection of debtor farmers which Daniel Shays had led just a few months earlier in western Massachusetts. Jefferson thought he saw, in every stitch of the new Constitution's fabric, the sign and token of that fear of popular unrest. His letters were full of reminders that the Shays episode was really a very isolated incident: one modest rebellion in one state over the eleven year life of the Articles of Confederation. Jefferson repeatedly argued that at this rate we would average one rebellion in each state every century and a half. "No country should be so long without one," he wrote to Madison.[2]

Shays' Rebellion was by no means the last time that a struggle between debtor farmers and city creditors would play a crucial role in the history of American public life. The next chapter, for example, addressing itself to a period one hundred years after the Constitution's birth, will focus on a presidential election which turned upon another struggle between debtor farmers and a largely city-based, commercial and industrial creditor class. Chapter 4, in a quick survey of modern problems of public policy in the West, identifies the farm crisis (a crisis which manifests itself most concretely in bank foreclosures of farms and ranches) as one of the central public policy issues of this place and time. The relationship between city and country, and the place of each in our political culture, has been a recurring problem in the history of American politics. Very often, the response to that problem has shaped public life much more profoundly than the problem itself seemed to warrant. That was certainly the case with Shays' Rebellion.

The delegates to the Constitutional Convention, and those who debated the proposed constitution in state assemblies, reverted time and again to that struggle in western Massachusetts between debtor farmers and a largely city-based, commercial creditor class. How should this struggle and others like it be worked out? The question came down to whether democratic citizens should be expected to work out the solution to such struggles directly among themselves or whether it is possible to adopt a machinery of government which would pump out solutions without requiring such direct citizen engagement. Should the burden of solving public problems rest most directly on citizenship or on government? In a letter to Madison in December of 1787, as the debate over the new Constitution was just beginning in the states, Jefferson raised that question as bluntly as one can imagine:

> And say, finally, whether peace is best preserved by giving energy to the government, or information to the people. This last is the most certain, and the most legitimate engine of government. Educate and inform the whole mass of the people. Enable them to see that it is their interest to preserve peace and order, and they will preserve them. . . . They are the only sure reliance for the preservation of our liberty.[3]

There is a tendency in our age to read Jeffersonian passages like this simply as panegyrics to public education. Indeed, Jefferson was praising education, but he had in mind a kind of civic or truly "public" education almost totally beyond our experience. Jefferson was speaking of education into citizenship, the heart of which was to enable people to see (and then act upon) the common good. It was this capacity on the part of large numbers of ordinary citizens to identify and pursue the common good which Jefferson argued needed to be brought to bear upon problems like those which underlay Shays' Rebellion. The "republican tradition" rested squarely upon this face-to-face, hands-on approach to problem-solving, with its implicit belief that people could rise above their particular interests to pursue a common good.

This republican approach to public policy required a high level of interaction among citizens. In particular, it assumed that citizens were presented with many opportunities and much encouragement to rise above a narrow self-centeredness. Only if citizens were, in various contexts, putting themselves in one another's shoes could they be expected to identify with and act upon a personally perceived vision of the common good. John Winthrop, the first colonial governor of Massachusetts, had spoken eloquently to his fellow Pilgrims of this need to put themselves in one another's shoes: "Wee must delight in eache other, make other's conditions our oune, rejoice together, mourne together, labour and suffer together, allwayes haveing before our eyes our commission and community in the worke as members of the same body." [4]

It was this attitude, this "making others' conditions our own," which was the object of public, or civic, education for Jefferson. People who had learned to "have before [their] eyes [their] community as members of the same body" would be in a position to "see that it is their interest to preserve peace and order" because it was in the interest of the "whole body" to preserve peace. Jefferson was trying to persuade Madison that reliance upon these "republican virtues" was the best way to deal with problems like those that underlay Shays' Rebellion. But he knew that, in fact, the Constitution rested less upon that republican foundation than upon a far different theory of government.

Republicanism was an intensive brand of politics; it was, heart and soul, a politics of engagement. It depended first upon people being deeply engaged with one another ("rejoicing and mourning, laboring and suffering together") and second upon citizens being directly and profoundly engaged with working out the solutions to public problems, by formulating and enacting the "common good." The federalist alternative to this republican politics of engagement was a politics of radical disengagement. The political theory which appeared in the *Federalist Papers* put far less weight than did republican theory either upon citizens being engaged with one another or upon their solving problems by formulating a vision of the common good. What the federalists proposed was to substitute for republican engagement two major alternative means of "insuring domestic tranquility." One of these means was a highly complex procedural machinery of checks and balances and mixed forms of government. The other was, quite simply, the western frontier. For the supporters of the Constitution, both the "procedural republic" and the frontier were essentially ways of avoiding the necessity (and what they saw as the instability) of the republican politics of engagement.[5] One very fruitful question for us to ask at the bicentennial of the Constitution and the centennial of the closing of the frontier is whether that twofold effort to escape has succeeded. But first, we need to understand more fully these two branches of the federalist solution.

The background, again, was Shays' Rebellion, along with other instances of what the framers identified as destabilizing "factionalism." Creditors and debtors, farmers and traders, slaveholders and abolitionists—the list of opposing factions seemed as endless as their potential to disrupt the stability of government and the even flow of commerce. The republicans urged education into "civic virtue" so that the creditor and the debtor could discern and act upon the common good. But what if these boisterous pupils destroyed the schoolhouse in the course of their education? How long would it take for civic virtue to take hold? Worse, what if the republican vision was only a daydream?

The great, hidden debate behind the Constitution was not about how to balance the interests of slave and free states, or of large and small states, but about the role of virtue, and of vice, as elements of citizenship. In the end, what emerged from the City of Brotherly Love was a view of human nature so gloomy that the cynical W. C. Fields could have embraced it wholeheartedly. Thomas Jefferson, on the other hand, could never be reconciled to it.

It was Jefferson's protege, James Madison, who presented the federalist view of human nature in its most unforgettable form. When the Constitution went to the states for ratification, the question of whether self-government could avoid constant rebellions arose with renewed furor. The *Federalist Papers*, written by Madison, Hamilton, and Jay in an effort to win support for the new Constitution, argued that instability could be minimized—not (as Jefferson argued) because people could be taught to be virtuous enough to rise above their particular interests sufficiently to pursue the common good, but because their vices could be effectively balanced against each other. The classic argument, in the tenth of the series of *Federalist Papers*, was penned by Madison:

> The latent causes of faction are . . . sown in the nature of man; and we see them everywhere brought into different degrees of activity according to the different circumstances of civil society. . . .
>
> It is in vain to say that enlightened statesmen will be able to adjust these clashing interests, and render them all subservient to the public good. . . .
>
> The inference to which we are brought is, that the *causes* of faction cannot be removed, and that relief is only to be sought in the means of controlling its *effects*.[6]

"The means of controlling its effects" consisted in the elaborate system of checks and balances and of mixed forms of government which the summer's labor in Philadelphia had produced. Instead of trusting in civic virtue as the main foundation of the new government, then, Madison and the other leading proponents of the Constitution rested their weight on what Madison called a "policy of supplying, by opposite and rival interests, the defect of better motives." Here is how Madison justified the Constitution's elaborate system of checks and balances: "It may be a reflection on human nature, that such devices should be necessary to control the abuses of government. But what is government itself, but the greatest of all reflections on human nature? If men were angels, no government would be necessary."[7]

It was precisely the classical republican faith in the ability of citizens to identify and act upon the common good which the Constitution's most fervent proponents found themselves unwilling to rely upon in the face of events like Shays' Rebellion. As a result, they launched a very different kind of government than many who had fought in the Revolution had bargained for. In *Reconstructing Public Policy*, William Sullivan describes this change:

> Madison, Hamilton, and the Federalists, fearful of the instability of republican governments, explicitly urged abandoning the language of civic virtue. They concentrated instead upon creating mechanisms to keep tyranny at bay without requiring common goals or institutions of intense popular participation. These developments had a fateful impact on political life and political discourse in America. The Federalist constitution of 1787 and the language of political mechanics it advanced together institutionalized the notion that politics is a business of balancing interests. . . . Where the civic republicans had emphasized conscious responsibility for the destiny of the political community, the Federalists emphasized the constitution as a framework which could protect the working of commercially competitive civil society."[8]

Republicans believed that public life was essentially a matter of the common choosing and willing of a common world—the "common unity" (or community), the "public thing" (or republic). The federalists argued that it was possible—in fact it was preferable—to carry on the most important public tasks without any such common willing of a common world. Individuals would pursue their private ends, and the structure of government would balance those pursuits so cleverly that the highest good would emerge without anyone having bothered to will its existence. It was no accident that this approach to public life was put forward by people who were centrally interested in creating optimal conditions for an expanding commercial and industrial economy. The federalist plan of government was exactly analogous to Adam Smith's invisible hand, which wrought the highest good in the market even though none of the actors were seeking anything beyond their own individual interest. Smith introduced the concept of the invisible hand into economics in 1776. Twelve years later, Madison introduced it into politics.[9]

With its advent in that realm, the *res* of the *res publica* lost its function. It, too, became invisible.

But the federalist rejection of republican principles did not stop with their negation of the common seeking of the common good. They also disagreed directly with traditional republican teaching about the proper scale of political organizations. Classical republican philosophy had always advocated small-scale units of government. Montesquieu, for example, had argued that the kind of self-government which rests upon civic virtue was only possible in small territories: "It is natural for a republic to have only a small territory; otherwise it cannot long subsist. . . . In an extensive republic the public good is sacrificed to a thousand private views; it is subordinate to exceptions, and depends on accidents. In a small one, the interest of the public is more obvious, better understood, and more within the reach of every citizen. . . ." [10]

Here, again, is the politics of engagement. Republics must be small so that people can be engaged with one another intensively and repeatedly enough to come to know and desire the common good. But already in 1787 this notion was problematic in the United States, if the primary political entity was to be the nation itself. This was, already, too large an arena for the intensive kind of face-to-face politics which republicanism represented.

It was, of all people, Alexander Hamilton who made this argument most forcefully to the Philadelphia convention. Three weeks into the debate on the Constitution, Hamilton made his first speech to the convention, outlining what he saw as the dangers of the proposals under discussion. After listing those dangers, he proceeded to a gloomy summary, which Madison duly reported: "This view of the subject almost led him to despair that a Republican Government could be established over so great an extent. He was sensible at the same time that it would be unwise to propose one of any other form." [11]

Unwise it may be to propose such a thing, but Hamilton was still willing to tell the delegates that in his opinion a government much closer to the British model, with an executive and upper house serving life tenure, was what was called for in a nation of "so great an extent." In other words, if a republic was not going to work in a nation of this size, then maybe what was needed was something besides a republic. This straightforward approach to Montesquieu's problem was not seriously entertained. Republican principles demanded lip service, if nothing more. In the end, Madison solved the problem by turning the "extensive territory" issue to advantage in exactly the same way that he proposed to turn the problem of self-interest to advantage—by making a virtue of what republicans had always considered an evil. An extensive territory, Madison argued, was an excellent hedge against tyranny—specifically against the "tyranny of the majority": "Extend the sphere, and you take in a greater variety of parties and interests; you make it less probable that a majority of the whole will have a common motive to invade the rights of other citizens; or if such a common motive exists, it will be more difficult for all who feel it to discover their own strengths and to act in unison with each other." [12]

Madison's reversal of the orthodox republican position on this issue is nothing short of breathtaking. Montesquieu had argued that a republic had to be small because only then could all the citizens gather around and get a good view of the "interest of the public"—of the "public thing." Like Arendt's table, that public thing had to be "within the reach of every citizen." The public interest can only emerge in this republican world if everyone is perceiving it and if everyone knows, because of proximity, that the others are perceiving it too. As Arendt says, "The term 'public' . . . means . . . that everything that appears in public can be seen and heard by everybody and has the widest possible publicity." [13] But Madison had abandoned the idea of citizens beholding, let alone acting upon, the public interest. It was their private interests which he wanted them to behold, to understand, and to pursue. And where Montesquieu needed to have each citizen see what the others saw, this would not do at all for Madison. If all those who were attached to a particular private interest learned that many others shared this attachment, the result might be the dreaded tyranny of the majority. But if the "republic" were spread over a broad enough territory, those who were attached to any given private interest would have much more difficulty finding out about each other, or forming a coalition. So where Montesquieu wanted people face to face and in touch with each other, Madison wanted them dispersed, disconnected, out of touch with each other. The republican principle demanded a small community where the citizens could simultaneously behold the "public thing." But the new American order required an "expanding sphere" precisely in order to keep people from too much beholding of a "common unity." What Rousseau had so painfully observed in theory was now being put into practice: "Keeping citizens apart has become the first maxim of modern politics."[14]

But if the federalists had discarded the basic principles of civic republicanism, they dared not jettison the language altogether. Too much blood had been spilled at the call of that language. Thus, in the article of the Constitution which addressed the admission of new states to the union, the framers included the following language: "The United States shall guarantee to every State in the Union a Republican Form of Government."[15] There was more than a little wordplay in this clause. Narrowly interpreted (as it always has been by the courts), the clause guaranteed nothing more than a representative, majoritarian structure of government. But the drafters well knew that by using the word *republican* they were appealing to the sentiments of many for whom that word had a much more substantial meaning. Those who had, in the summer of 1776, pledged "their lives, their fortunes, and their sacred honor" to the republican cause were now especially interested in the guarantee of republicanism to the states. Many of them saw clearly enough that the Constitution had largely abandoned reliance upon civic virtue in the case of the national government, but they still believed (or believed even more fervently) that such principles must be kept vital in the states. To these republican stalwarts the guarantee to the states of a "republican form of government" was no mere formality.

But in guaranteeing a republican government to the states, the Constitution was also bowing to Madison's notion of "extending the sphere." The republican government clause appears in the context of the Constitution's discussion of how new states shall be admitted to the Union. As the Constitution faces westward, then, it strikes a profoundly ambivalent posture, torn, as it were, between the political principles of federalism ("extending the sphere") and republicanism (guaranteeing a "republican government" to those entitites—the states—which were small enough to *be* republics). This ambivalence becomes even more profound if we turn from Madison's to Jefferson's view of the frontier.

When Madison spoke of "extending the sphere," he was forecasting a reality which both Madison and Jefferson would find themselves confronting during their presidencies, as America's "manifest destiny" unfolded. It was Jefferson, of course, who extended the sphere farther than anyone else with his constitutionally suspect acquisition of the Louisiana Purchase. But even as he looked westward, Jefferson saw not the Madisonian balancing of interests, not a way of "keeping citizens apart," but the republican building of civic virtue. Jefferson wanted to extend the frontier because for him the "expanding sphere" was the best way to assure the continued vitality of republican principles. In that same letter to Madison, written from Paris in the waning days of 1787, Jefferson identified tersely where he thought self-government in America must remain rooted: "This reliance [upon the people] cannot deceive us, as long as we remain virtuous, and I think we shall be so, as long as agriculture is our principal object, which will be the case, while there remains vacant lands in any part of America."[16]

As long as there was new land to expand into, agriculture would continue to be the main occupation of Americans. This, in turn, would maintain civic virtue as a central force in American political culture. This linking of civic virtue to farming, and the further linking of the ascendancy of agriculture to the availability of open land, was not a passing fancy with Jefferson. In 1785 he had written on the same subject to John Jay: "We have now lands enough to employ an infinite number of people in their cultivation. Cultivators of the earth are the most valuable citizens. They are the most vigorous, the most independent, the most virtuous, and they are tied to their country, and wedded to its liberty and interests, by the most lasting bonds." [17]

Earlier, during the war, after commenting again upon the availability of new land, Jefferson had gone well beyond calling farmers "the most valuable citizens": "Those who labor in the earth are the chosen people of God, if ever He had a chosen people, whose breasts He has made His peculiar deposit for substantial and genuine virtue. It is the focus in which he keeps alive that sacred fire, which otherwise might escape from the face of the earth." [18]

Behind what we might now regard as a touch of overzealousness on this point lies an important, if controversial, principle of public philosophy. In all these reflections about the connection between civic virtue and agriculture, Jefferson was contrasting agriculture (and specifically subsistence agriculture) to commerce and to manufacturing. What bothered him about those nonfarming activities was the disconnectedness and the anonymity which seemed necessarily to accompany them. Jefferson saw clearly that those who made their living through these activities were wholly dependent upon the choices of utter strangers, known only as "consumers." This, he argued time and again, led to the undermining of morals, and particularly of civic virtue, in sharp contrast to the situation of farmers, who grew their own food and fiber:

> Corruption of morals in the mass of cultivators is a phenomenon of which no age nor nation has furnished an example. It is the mark set on those, who, not looking up to heaven, to their own soil [toil?] and industry, as does the husbandman, for their subsistence, depend for it on casualties and caprice of customers. Dependence begets subservi-

ence and venality, suffocates the germ of virtue, and prepares fit tools
for the designs of ambition.[19]

A key phrase here is the "casualties and caprice of customers."
Jefferson was appalled by the thought of large numbers of people
making their living by depending solely upon the choices of other
people with whom they had no social or moral ties of any kind. Yet
it was this very disconnectedness which lay at the heart of Adam
Smith's doctrine of the "invisible hand" of the market. It was
precisely because consumers were totally autonomous from producers, precisely because they were acting solely upon their own "caprice," that the market worked in such a marvelous way. And it was
the same nameless, faceless nature of the far-flung, diverse national
polity upon which Madison pinned his hopes for the new Constitution. "Keeping citizens apart," disconnected, anonymous, was the
Madisonian formula for stability. Any sense of responsibility for one
another was as little necessary to citizenship under Madison's constitution as it was to the market dealings of Smith's consumers and
producers.

But Jefferson, like John Winthrop, believed that a sense of mutual
responsibility for one another was a necessary feature of self-
government. He believed that the way people made their livings had
much to do with the development of such a sense of responsibility,
and that farming developed it most consistently. Farmers who were
primarily engaged in feeding, clothing, and housing their own families had no choice but to depend upon their own skill and industry.
In this (the weather notwithstanding) there was nothing capricious;
there was no way to fool anyone about anything; "designs and
ambition" would not answer. In the hard, direct necessities of such
agriculture, Jefferson saw the roots of a plain honesty, industry, and
perseverance—he saw, in other words, the roots of those "civic
virtues" upon which real citizenship depended.

Jefferson saw clearly that the new Constitution, as Madison had
presented it, placed precious little reliance upon such civic virtues.

Because of that, he worried that the Constitution marked a major retreat from the republican principles which had always been so important to him, and for which he believed the war had been fought. But if the new nation seemed like a retreat from republican principles, Jefferson could take comfort in the Constitution's guarantee to the states of a "republican form of government." He could foresee that the vast, open lands of the frontier would be at once a source of new states, and that those states would be republican in the most fundamental sense because open lands would draw people into agriculture, at least as fast as they were drawn into cities and factories. Republican principles would thrive "as long as agriculture is our principal object, which will be the case, while there remains vacant lands in any part of America."

But clearly, the Jeffersonian dream must fade or change over time. It depends upon farmers pouring into open land faster than people "pile up in cities." But farmers settling open land must sooner or later settle all of it. Jefferson sometimes seemed to try to hide this fact from himself by speaking of there being "lands enough to employ an infinite number of people in their cultivation." But even the vast American frontier could not be *that* vast. In fact, just a century after Jefferson wrote that letter to Madison, the most remote region of the Louisiana Purchase had been admitted to the union, with each of the new states duly guaranteed a "Republican Form of Government." But the admission of these states also marked the closing of the old American frontier. What, then, would become of Jefferson's equation of republican virtue with the continued existence of open land?

Madison spoke of "extending the sphere" as a way of "keeping people apart," which may be seen as a way of escaping the necessity of citizens facing each other and solving their problems directly among themselves. Both Madison's mechanistic view of government and his view of the role of the frontier can (and in later chapters will) be criticized as being, in a sense, escapist—as simply deferring an inevitable kind of facing up to each other. But much the same could be said of Jefferson's view of the frontier. Particularly if we keep Shays' Rebellion in mind, as one in a long series of skirmishes between agrarians and city-dwellers, we could well conclude that Jefferson's way of thinking of the frontier was simply a means of postponing the inevitable facing into each other of these two great social and political forces. The next chapter will explore how the closing of the frontier brought that confrontation to a climax.

What Jefferson was arguing, of course, was that the ideal of republicanism itself depended upon the continued existence of open land into which agriculture could expand. Insofar as civic virtues are more effectively transmitted in rural than in urban settings, Jefferson's argument deserves careful attention. Yet it is worth noting that from across the Atlantic came a precisely opposite view of the relationship between the American frontier and the development of civic culture. During the 1820s, as America became transfixed on its manifest destiny, Hegel had argued that until America had settled down, it would remain incapable of any real civil society. Hegel's perspective was, point for point, the precise opposite of Jefferson's. Hegel recognized that America was nominally much more "republican" than any country in Europe, but he argued that in fact the "public" of the *res publica* was almost totally lacking here:

> If we compare North America further with Europe, we shall find in the former the permanent example of a republican constitution. A subjective unity presents itself: for there is a president at the head of the state, who, for the sake of security against any monarchical ambition, is chosen only for four years. Universal protection for property, and a something approaching entire immunity from public burdens, are facts which are constantly held up to commendation. We have in these facts the fundamental character of the community—the endeavor of the individual after acquisition, commercial profit, and gain; the preponderance of *private* interest, devoting itself to that of the community only for its own advantage.[20]

Hegel attributed the absence of a true civic culture in part to the lack of sharp class distinctions, but of even greater importance in his analysis was the escape valve of the frontier:

As to the political condition of North America, the general object of the existence of this state is not yet fixed and determined, and the necessity for a firm combination does not yet exist; for a real state and a real government arise only . . . when such a condition of things presents itself that a large portion of the people can no longer satisfy its necessities in the way in which it has been accustomed so to do. But America is hitherto exempt from this pressure, for it has the outlet of colonization constantly and widely open, and multitudes are continually streaming into the plains of the Mississippi. By this means the chief source of discontent is removed, and the continuation of the existing civil condition is guaranteed.[21]

So where Jefferson had foreseen the continued vitality of republican principles "while there remains vacant lands in any part of America," Hegel argued that a real republic would become possible in America "only after the immeasurable space which that country presents to its inhabitants shall have been occupied, and the members of the political body shall have begun to be pressed back on each other." And Hegel even contradicted Jefferson on the issue of the role of rural and city economies in civic life: "Only when, as in Europe, the direct increase of agriculturists is checked, will the inhabitants, instead of pressing outwards to occupy the fields, press inwards upon each other—pursuing town occupations, and trading with their fellow-citizens; and so form a compact system of civil society, and require an organized state."[22]

By the time that the last of Jefferson's Louisiana Purchase had been settled enough for admission into the Union, the process of "pressing inwards upon each other" had finally begun in earnest. What would this mean for "republican forms of government?"

Notes

1. Thomas Jefferson to John Adams, November 13, 1787, in *The Papers of Thomas Jefferson*, Vol. XII, pp. 350–51.
2. Thomas Jefferson to James Madison, December 20, 1787, in *The Papers of Thomas Jefferson*, Vol. XII, p. 478.

3. Ibid.

4. John Winthrop, "A Modell of Christian Charity," written on board the *Arbella* on the Atlantic Ocean in 1630, in *Collections of the Massachusetts Historical Society*, Vol. 27, p. 47.

5. The phrase *procedural republic* is from an article by Michael J. Sandel, "The Procedural Republic and the Unencumbered Self," *Political Theory* 12 (February, 1984): 81–96.

6. James Madison, "Federalist Paper No. 10," in Alexander Hamilton, James Madison, and John Jay, *The Federalist Papers*, p. 79.

7. James Madison, "Federalist Paper No. 51," in ibid., p. 322.

8. William M. Sullivan, *Reconstructing Public Philosophy*, p. 12.

9. By this I mean that Madison's politics were *laissez-faire*, in that they did not rely upon the classical republican *telos* of the common good, just as Smith's economics dispensed with such a commonly perceived good. I do not mean to imply that Madison's economics were entirely *laissez-faire*.

10. Charles, Baron de Montesquieu, *The Spirit of Laws*, Book VIII, Chapter XVI, p. 130.

11. James Madison, *Debates in the Federal Convention of 1787*, p. 134.

12. Madison, "Federalist Paper No. 10," p. 83.

13. Hannah Arendt, *The Human Condition*, p. 50.

14. This passage from Jean Jacques Rousseau is quoted by Michael Ignatieff in *The Needs of Strangers*, p. 105.

15. United States Constitution, Article IV, Section 4.

16. Thomas Jefferson to James Madison, December 20, 1787, in *The Papers of Thomas Jefferson*, Vol. XII, pp. 478–79.

17. Thomas Jefferson to John Jay, August 23, 1785, in *The Papers of Thomas Jefferson*, Vol. VIII, p. 426.

18. Thomas Jefferson, *Notes on the State of Virginia*, Query XIX, p. 157.

19. Ibid.

20. Georg Wilhelm Friedrich Hegel, *The Philosophy of History*, pp. 84–85.

21. Ibid., pp. 85–86.

22. Ibid., p. 86.

CHAPTER THREE

The Descending Horizon

"As long as there remain vacant lands in any part of America." In 1889, just over a century after Jefferson wrote those words to Madison, the vast stretches of Montana and the Dakotas were deemed to be populated enough to justify the admission of three new states to the Union. A year later, Wyoming and Idaho were admitted, and in that same year (1890), the constitutionally mandated decennial census was taken. In 1893, when the results of that census had been analyzed, a young historian delivered a paper to the American Historical Association meeting in Chicago. Frederick Jackson Turner opened his remarks by referring to the recently completed census:

> In a recent bulletin of the Superintendent of the Census for 1890 appear these significant words: "Up to and including 1880 the country had a frontier of settlement, but at present the unsettled area has been so broken into by isolated bodies of settlement that there can hardly be said to be a frontier line. In the discussion of its extent, its westward movement, etc., it can not, therefore, any longer have a place in the census reports." This brief official statement marks the closing of a great historic movement. Up to our own day American history has

been in a large degree the history of the colonization of the Great West. The existence of an area of free land, its continuous recession, and the advance of American settlement westward, explain American development.[1]

Like Jefferson, Turner saw "the existence of an area of free land" as a very important feature of the American political landscape. Indeed, just as Jefferson had spoken of "vacant lands" in a letter which addressed the possibility of republican government under the new Constitution, Turner also, a century later, related the issue of open land to the Constitution: "Behind institutions, behind constitutional forms and modifications, lie the vital forces that call these organs into life and shape them to meet changing conditions. The peculiarity of American institutions is, the fact that they have been compelled to adapt themselves to the changes of an expanding people—to the changes involved in crossing a continent, in winning a wilderness. . . ."[2]

What Turner was saying, in effect, was that one could not understand the first century of American constitutional history apart from the existence of the frontier. But he was also saying that the next century of constitutional history would have to be a different matter—simply because there was no longer a frontier: "And now, four centuries from the discovery of America, at the end of a hundred years of life under the Constitution, the frontier has gone, and with its going has closed the first period of American history."[3]

Jefferson had been concerned about the continued existence of open land, because in it he saw the best hope for the continued vitality of republican principles. Turner made the same connection, illustrating it with this quote from a frontier orator speaking in 1830:

"But, sir, it is not the increase of population in the West which this gentleman ought to fear. It is the energy which the mountain breeze and western habits impart to these emigrants. They are regenerated, politically I mean, sir. They soon become *working politicians*; and the difference, sir, between a *talking* and a *working* politician is immense. The Old Dominion has long been celebrated for producing great orators; the ablest metaphysicians in policy; men that can split hairs in all abstruse questions of political economy. But at home, or when they return from Congress, they have negroes to fan them asleep. But a [frontier] statesman, though far inferior in logic, metaphysics, and rhetoric to an old Virginia statesman, has this advantage, that when he returns home he takes off his coat and takes hold of his plow. This gives him bone and muscle, sir, and preserves his republican principles pure and uncontaminated."[4]

Here, then, we find this word *republican* used, not in an abstract, constitutional context, but in connection to the sweaty and dusty business of holding a hand-plow in the ground. The precise nature of that connection may still seem a little mysterious, but if Jefferson and this unnamed frontier orator were in any sense correct in making that connection, then the Constitution's guarantee of "a republican form of government" to the states should have been secure enough in the early 1890s. Those five states which had just been admitted offered more than their share of the kind of political education which came at the end of a plow. If it was eating dust that would guarantee republicanism, these new states were certainly entering the union on a solid republican footing.

But if Turner (or for that matter Jefferson) was right, things would no longer be the same now that the frontier was closed. Specifically, the preservation of "republican principles" would be far less certain, now that the "area of open land" was settled. Yet even as Turner wrote, America was witnessing the expansion of a movement whose republican principles were as pure as anything Jefferson could have prescribed. And this movement, which has come to be associated with the term *populism*, was based precisely where Jefferson had thought that republicanism would always have to be based: on the farm. This agrarian populist movement was at its height, and indeed appeared to be on the verge of grasping national power, at the very moment that Turner declared the frontier closed. Republican principles appeared to be on the march, not in the kind of retreat that Turner's analysis would seem to imply. Yet with the election of 1896, this great Jeffersonian movement suffered a defeat from which it never recovered.

Like any presidential election, the 1896 contest between William Jennings Bryan and William McKinley can legitimately be portrayed in any number of ways. Perhaps no election has ever so clearly pitted against each other the forces which Thomas Jefferson identified as the key elements in American politics. The agrarian populist movement ("those who labor in the earth") furnished the great, fervent core of Bryan's support, while a new consolidation of commercial and manufacturing interests characterized McKinley's winning effort. The populist movement had risen steadily in power until it was in a position to give Bryan both the Democratic and the Populist party nominations. But rising to meet this wave, under the able direction of Ohio industrialist Mark Hanna, there appeared a fusing of moneyed interests and mass communication technology which was to transform American politics in a lasting way. Lawrence Goodwyn, a leading historian of the populist movement, describes the transformation in terms which reverberate to our own time: "The 1896 campaign had to do with the mobilization of new customs that were to live much more securely in American politics than the dreams of the Populists. . . . The most visible difference in the efforts of the three parties in 1896 turned on money—not as a function of currency, but rather as the essential ingredient of modern electioneering." [5]

It was not just the infusion of unprecedented *amounts* of money in the campaign that inaugurated the modern era; the money was also *used* in a new and lasting way. This was the campaign which made Madison Avenue a permanent and central feature in American politics: "The corporate contributions mobilized in behalf of the 1896 Republican campaign for McKinley financed America's first concentrated mass advertising campaign aimed at organizing the minds of the American people on the subject of political power, who should have it, and why. . . . In sheer depth, the advertising campaign organized by Mark Hanna in behalf of William McKinley was without parallel in American history. It set creative standards for the twentieth century." [6]

The populists had built their power by teaching people new methods of cooperation, both in economics and in politics. In a variety of ways, this movement had brought people face to face with each other so that they could work out, among themselves, the possibilities of a better way of life. People within the movement had learned to depend upon each other, to trust each other, to educate each other. In all of these ways, the populist movement depended upon precisely those "civic virtues" and republican principles of face-to-face politics which had been so important to Americans from John Winthrop to Thomas Jefferson. But in the end, the Populists were defeated by a system which relied, not upon those face-to-face dealings, but upon the highly impersonal methods of mass communication.

It was almost as if Jefferson and Madison had been in a race to the end of the frontier. Jefferson had always seen industrialization as the gravest threat to real self-government, and he looked to the frontier, to its capacity to keep agriculture growing as fast as manufacturing, as the best safeguard of self-government. As the open land filled up, the farmers, now as strong as they would ever be, made their best effort to reclaim their republic. The new states, where "mountain breezes and Western habits" prevailed, did their part. Of eight states that had been admitted to the union since 1888, seven supported Bryan. But in the end, at the closing of the old frontier, Jefferson and his farmers lost the race. Whether Madison won or not, Madison Avenue certainly did. Goodwyn describes the outcome as at once a victory for the new methods of persuasion and a decisive setback for the principles of self-government: "A critical cultural battle had been lost by those who cherished the democratic ethos. . . . The demonstrated effectiveness of the new political methods of mass advertising meant, in effect, that the cultural values of the corporate state were politically unassailable in twentieth-century America." [7]

It was not, according to Goodwyn, simply that one interest had won out against another. The fundamental faith of ordinary people in their ability to govern themselves had been lastingly diminished: "Increasingly, the modern condition of "the people" is illustrated by their general acquiescence in their own political inability to affect their governments in substantive ways. Collective political resignation is a constant of public life in the technological societies of the twentieth century." Finally, the range of what we even mean by politics, or by public life, was diminished as well: "Older aspirations—dreams of achieving a civic culture grounded in generous social relations and in a celebration of the vitality of human cooperation and the diversity of human aspiration itself—have come to seem so out of place in the twentieth century societies of progress that the mere recitation of such longings, however authentic they have always been, now constitutes a social embarrassment." [8]

Goodwyn speaks of contemporary politics in terms of "a clear retreat from the democratic vistas of either the eighteenth-century Jeffersonians or the nineteenth-century Populists." [9] Jefferson would not have been at all surprised to hear that political horizons had begun to contract noticeably just as the ever-receding horizon of the frontier was also closed off. Jefferson's farmers—his "most virtuous citizens" could not endlessly expand into new territory. Commercial and industrial forces were bound to overtake the pioneer agrarian expansion. When that happened, Jeffersonian republicanism was certain to be set back.

But if we view the frontier from Hegel's as well as Jefferson's perspective, the story becomes more complicated. Hegel, remember, saw the frontier as an escape valve, delaying the time when America's social and economic forces would have to face one another and reach some form of accommodation. It was only then, Hegel had argued, that a genuinely civil state would become necessary (or indeed possible) in America.

If the frontier had closed by 1890, then perhaps America was ready to start facing into itself in the way that Hegel had predicted. But, whether coincidentally or not, the last few years of the century brought the nation two new escape valves, which in a sense replaced the frontier and allowed a further delay in the development of what Hegel had identified as civic culture. The first of these developments was the new, extracontinental phase of American imperialism. The second was to become the unique contribution of the twentieth century to "public life": the launching of the regulatory bureaucracy.

In 1886, Theodore Roosevelt left behind his Dakota Territory adventure in Wild West ranching; by 1898, his Rough Riders were charging up San Juan Hill. By then, North Dakota had become a state, and Cuba, a colony. (Within twenty years, many North Dakotans had concluded that there was little difference between the two.) America (if there had ever been any doubt about it) had become an empire. From at least the first century B.C., when the Roman Republic became the Roman Empire, there had been good reason to doubt whether empires could ever also be republics. As America turned its attention from settling a continent to becoming a world power, these doubts took root and grew in many American minds. Robinson Jeffers, for example, began his poem "Shine, Perishing Republic" by observing that America was losing its republican heritage as it found itself "heavily thickening to empire." [10]

The growth of empire undermines republican possibilities in subtle but fundamental ways. One of the unspoken purposes of imperial expansion is often to postpone the necessity of facing, head-on and decisively, the task of accommodating indigenous social and economic forces to each other. Jingoism and flag-waving unite those forces, at least on the surface, enabling them to ignore or gloss over those differences which Hegel said had, eventually, to be confronted. So America entered the twentieth century with the old frontier closed, but with a new escape valve in its place.

But not just one escape valve. The waning years of the nineteenth century also introduced another substantial means of avoiding the development of an intentional, intensive civic culture. In 1887, Congress passed the Interstate Commerce Act, creating the Interstate Commerce Commission and launching the new age of regulatory bureaucracy. Chapter 5 will explore the effect of this new departure on civic virtue and republican self-government. To anticipate briefly, the argument will be that regulatory bureaucracy represents a major development in the modern project of "keeping citizens apart"—shielding them from the necessity of direct, face-to-face (republican) problem-solving. Even though the "expanding sphere" of the frontier had closed, the necessity of facing toward one another could still be delayed through a more intensive development of the second federalist escape valve: the "procedural republic."

Corporate domination, empire, the growth of regulatory bureaucracy: the closing of the nineteenth century and of the old frontier seemed indeed to have weakened substantially the republican foundations of the nation. In many ways, the political history of the intervening century has been a story of the consolidation of those antirepublican trends. Yet even now, two centuries after the Constitution was debated and adopted, a century after the frontier closed, more and more people are speaking of the need for a renewal of civic culture, often couching their call in explicitly republican terms. There seems to be nothing strictly linear about this story; it keeps looping back on itself. This becomes even clearer if we sharpen our focus from civic culture generally to its development within one specific area—that region whose settlement marked the closing of the old American frontier.

Notes

1. Frederick Jackson Turner, *The Frontier in American History*, p. 1.
2. Ibid., p. 2.
3. Ibid., p. 38.
4. Ibid., p. 31.
5. Lawrence Goodwyn, *The Populist Moment*, p. 278.
6. Ibid., pp. 280, 282.
7. Ibid., p. 290.

8. Ibid., p. 291, 292.
9. Ibid., p. 265.
10. Robinson Jeffers, "Shine, Perishing Republic," in *The Selected Poetry of Robinson Jeffers*, p. 168. Jeffers' republicanism was much more of the Jeffersonian than the Hegelian variety. Consider this stanza from the same poem:

> But for my children, I would have them keep their distance from
>   the thickening center; corruption
> Never has been compulsory, when the cities lie at the monster's
>   feet there are left the mountains.

CHAPTER FOUR

The Empty Quarter and the Vanishing Public

When Ted Schwinden was sworn in as governor of Montana in January of 1981, he spoke of this part of the nation as comprising "the last of what is best in America." Schwinden had campaigned and won on the slogan "straight talk—good people," and the plain-spoken, uncomplicated neighborliness of his constituents was part of what he characterized as the last of what is best in America. Another part—a big part—was the open space, the range and power of the land. In fact, what the new governor evoked in speaking of "the last of what is best in America" was the old image of the American frontier, both in the feel of the land and the way of the people.

Whether the frontier was in fact the "best" feature of American history or not, it has undeniably been a dominant feature and a major determinant of America's destiny and identity. To speak, then, of "the last of what is best in America" is not only a matter of indulging the vanity of the people who live out here; it also calls to mind some deeply American questions. The common theme of those questions has to do with how America treats the last of its relatively open country. How much of its wilderness will America preserve

35

here? What, if anything, will the nation do to protect the family farm? How will federal policy affect the use and distribution of the millions of acre feet of water that arise in these headwaters? How genuinely will we respect the sovereignty of the Indian tribes whose presence always had to be ignored or overcome in order to call this "open land" at all? How many and what kinds of missiles will the nation deploy here, precisely because the country is still so open and relatively devoid of people?

Even if the nation did not face these and other questions about what to do with its "empty quarter,"[1] the frontier would still remain as an American issue. The frontier experience has been so utterly central to the American identity that even if the nation wanted simply to forget the frontier and move ahead without reference to it, the likelihood of success would be about the same as that of a young adult who one day decided that she would live the rest of her life without reference to or influence from any of the joys and tribulations of her earlier years. Such rejection of the influence of the past is no more possible for a people or a civilization than it is for an individual.

In fact, if we shift our attention from the national-historical to the individual level, it becomes even more evident that the frontier image cannot simply be ignored. If you ask residents of this region—especially those who clearly remember their arrival here—why they are here and not somewhere else, you hear time and again the story of feeling crowded, oppressed, and alienated elsewhere. These people speak of the need they felt to be able to get into open country, to experience its power, to come to know and identify themselves against the background of such a setting. The experience of being drawn into and claimed by open country, which John McPhee captures perfectly in the Alaskan phrase "coming into the country,"[2] was the essence of the frontier, but it is also the essence of why most of us live "way out here." If that is so, then it surely must be a mistake to treat the frontier experience as something lying entirely in our past. For many inhabitants of this region, their very sense of identity, and certainly their sense of place, is deeply connected to the frontier experience. Whether we view the notion of "the last of what is best in America" from the perspective of the nation, then, or from the perspective of those who live in this region, we are drawn inevitably to think about the frontier past of this headwaters region, but also, and more importantly, about its future. What role will this region and its residents play in the next phase of American history?

There seem to be three or four main possibilities. The likeliest answer is that the last arena of a way of life based on open country will disappear as the rest of it has, under the ever-less-gradual industrialization and urbanization of the continent. Every long-range economic forecast documents America's accelerating demand for this region's resources. What is remarkable about that demand is that, coming as late as it does in the history of America's geometrically accelerating industrialization, it promises to occur on a scale never yet witnessed. The largest strip mines or metal mines, the largest power lines, the largest pipelines, and later, perhaps, the largest layoffs in history await the development of these most remote of the Lower Forty-Eight's resources. Our remoteness itself often exacerbates this matter of scale. If you are going to carry electricity thousands of miles from mine-mouth coal-fired plants, it makes no sense to build small plants or modest powerlines. Alaska (America's real "last frontier") is instructive: the size of the Alaska pipeline is directly related to the remoteness of Prudhoe Bay from any markets for its petroleum.

Remoteness has another side effect which in a sense carries to its logical conclusion this first and gloomiest forecast of the region's future. "Underpopulated," remote, and therefore half-forgotten in the scheme of American politics, this region has become the logical place for the nation to deploy large numbers of its nuclear warheads, with their unerring capacity to attract their opposite numbers. Along with the pipelines and strip mines, then, this land has also had to bear one of the largest concentrations of deadly force in the world's history. This dire presence may well prove to be the ultimate, sudden, and final determinant of the region's future. One way or another, by industrialization or incineration, the last glimmer of the frontier seems likely to pass.

For most of the region's inhabitants, that outcome, in any of its manifestations, is profoundly unacceptable. That being so, we have to return to the question of what it means to live in a remote and lightly populated region, if not simply to witness its demise. When Ted Schwinden spoke of "the last of what is best in America," he sounded, among other things, a note of nostalgia to which most of us are at some moments prone—a desire to stop the clock, if not to turn it back. Such a return to the past might be thought of as the second possible fate of the region. There are those who, in one form or another, would chart that course. But while many of us may sometimes dream of reliving days gone by, we share a suspicion, bordering on conviction, that this is not to be, that whatever the significance of "the last of what is best" may be, it cannot be a matter of turning the clock back. While we must understand and preserve what is best from the past, we must also openly engage change, seeking to guide it, not to stop it.

If annihilation of open country and its accompanying way of life is unconscionable, and if nostalgic preservation is naive, we have to consider middle courses. A third scenario, then, is for people of good will to continue valiantly to resist the worst incursions on their way of life, to continue to strive, individually or through pluralistic coalitions, to move society toward a better future. This approach has been a substantial feature of the political history of this region since the early seventies, and it has clearly made a difference in the course of events. The question is whether this way of dealing with "the last of what is best" is good enough. The fact is that most of the victories claimed through this kind of struggle are victories only in the sense that things might have been worse. It is a victory when we slow or scale down a threat to our way of life, but all too rarely do we actually gain ground.

What is worse, the way our political system leads us to pursue our visions very often has the effect of alienating more and more people from public life altogether. The region's "public interest" movement has gained great skill and sophistication over the past decade and a half and has won many important battles on behalf of a better life for the people of the region. Yet here, just as in other regions of the country, citizen apathy is spreading steadily, and, strangely enough, it is worsened by nearly every important struggle for a better way of life within the region. This is a painfully paradoxical situation. How can the public interest possibly thrive if the very battles fought in its name leave fewer and fewer people willing to be "public" at all?

Consider the example of public land, and particularly wild lands. The Northern Rockies states all have vast stretches of federally owned land, and for over a decade now they, and the nation itself, have been embroiled in a seemingly endless process of deciding how much of that land to designate as protected wilderness. That debate pits various interests (environmental, recreational, agricultural, mining interests) against each other in a standoff struggle which has sapped the energy and resources of all concerned. At the same time, this struggle has gradually undermined nearly all parties' faith that the process of public decision making is in fact capable of identifying or producing the public interest.

If we turn our attention from wild land to farmland, similar frustrations emerge. This is a region where family farms and a small-town, rural way of life have long been central to the residents' sense of identity and their vision of the good life. Over the years, the nation, too, has affirmed these values, mostly in words and images, but often in deeds as well. But since the early 1980s, family farms have suffered a rate of bankruptcy and foreclosure which threatens to weaken drastically, if not to destroy, that valued rural way of life. What is our public response to this tragedy? Do we as a nation really care? Or is such caring a publicly irrelevant concept? Should the public stance instead be a stoic one of allowing the market to weed out the "inefficient operators?" Such questions matter deeply to the people of this region. We are divided by them, and we are frustrated by our national inability to answer them in any satisfactory way. Once again, that frustration translates subtly but steadily into a weakening of our democratic faith.

As rural livelihoods become less of an option in the region, the pressure steadily mounts to create other kinds of jobs, and in every instance this, too, raises questions about how we act as a body politic. Resource-rich and people-poor, this region has always had to deal with proposals for gigantic developments (ranging today from complexes of gargantuan mines, power plants, and transmission lines to proposals for deploying MX and Midgetman missiles). These mammoth projects offer jobs to economies which sorely need them; they also offer vast disruptions to what remains of a rural way of life. So the people of the region are constantly faced with the question of how far they should go in trying to protect a valued way of life, as opposed to creating a "climate" which encourages these job-creating activities. These issues almost always present either/or, win/lose choices; they evoke polarization and heated rhetoric; they abound in delays and hearings and rehearings. Sometimes someone wins for a while, but almost always we all lose in the sense that more citizens are thrown into despair and alienation—into a feeling that we have ourselves so tied in knots that none of us can do anything.

Citizen alienation, wilderness and farm policy, economic development strategies: all of these topics and dozens of others call into question the way that we in this nation and this region go about the business of being public. Voter apathy is a matter of a deepening denial of our capacity for, or our interest in, being public at all. Wildland issues raise the question of how we publicly decide to manage public land. Farm policy raises the issue of how we publicly choose to rank our values. Economic development issues raise recurrent problems about the relationship between public regulations and private enterprise.

These place-specific issues only serve to remind us of how ubiquitous our use of the word *public* is at the very time that we seem to be losing our capacity to deal with these issues in an effectively "public" way. As we consider issues like open land and agriculture against this background, we naturally recall Jefferson's insistence that an effective self-governing "public" depended upon both agriculture and open land. Jefferson advanced that argument from a position of severe doubt about what the new form of American government was going to mean for the future of public life. In the end, of course, the point is not what Jefferson thought, but what we now can, should, and will do with that part of the world we call home.

But what "we" do depends upon who "we" are (or who we think we are). It depends, in other words, upon how we choose to relate to each other, to the place we inhabit, and to the issues which that inhabiting raises for us. All of those "we" questions are about our way of being public. Our current way of doing that is not satisfactory—or at least it is not satisfying the needs or aspirations of a growing number of people. My own experience in public life, dealing with the kinds of issues mentioned here, has left me convinced that our way of being public is a deepening failure. I also believe that Jefferson was right—that we cannot successfully fashion ourselves as a "public" until we replace that word within its "republican" context, and within the context of the way we inhabit very particular stretches of land. If in fact there is a connection between the places we inhabit and the political culture which our inhabiting of them produces, then perhaps it makes sense to begin with the place, with a sense of what it is, and then try to imagine a way of being public which would fit the place.

There is perhaps no better way to get a sense of what *this* place is than to ask why it (and not someplace else) became the last of that old frontier. There were good reasons that this dry, windy, cold, hot, remote region was so late in being settled. Those features still keep the region largely unpopulated. This, in turn, preserves the sense that the land is dominant here—that this is a place of more

land than people. It seems to come naturally, then, that people tend
to define themselves in terms of the land that surrounds them. This
is a step in the direction of answering the question of public identity—the question of who "we" are. But given the background of
the American frontier, it remains only a tentative step in that direction. Even when people define themselves against the background
of a dominant landscape, there remains the possibility of a very
substantial ambivalence about the particulars of that definition. In
The Sound of Mountain Water, Wallace Stegner acknowledges that
ambivalence and speaks forcefully (and, I am convinced, correctly)
about how it should be resolved:

> There will be some continuing open space. Not all the immigration
> of the next hundred years, as the continent fills and overflows, can do
> more than overcrowd the oases: the arid backlands will remain essen-
> tially unpeopled. . . . [T]here will be enough of the old wild undamaged
> country left to give us the smell of sagebrush wetted by a shower, the
> bitter tang of mountain aspen, the smoke of juniper or piñon fires:
> western smells. . . .
>
> Angry as one may be at what heedless men have done and still do to
> a noble habitat, one cannot be pessimistic about the West. This is the
> native home of hope. When it fully learns that cooperation, not rugged
> individualism, is the quality that most characterizes and preserves it,
> then it will have achieved itself and outlived its origins. Then it has a
> chance to create a society to match its scenery.[3]

If neither a nostalgic return to "the good old days" nor annihilation of a way of life based on open country are appropriate or
acceptable futures for this region, and if the continuation of a politics
of polarization will only weaken still further our capacity for an
effective public life, then perhaps it is time to hear again Stegner's
call to cooperation as the region's best chance to "create a society
to match its scenery." I will argue in later chapters that Stegner's
formula is of a piece with the contemporary resurgence of interest
in those republican principles which Jefferson identified so closely

with open country. But before we can seriously consider how it might be feasible to follow Stegner's advice, it is important to understand in more detail how far we have journeyed from those republican roots.

Notes

1. See Joel Garreau, *The Nine Nations of North America*.
2. See John McPhee, *Coming into the Country*.
3. Wallace Stegner, *The Sound of Mountain Water*, pp. 37–38.

CHAPTER FIVE

Stalemate

Wallace Stegner urges the West to learn that "cooperation, not rugged individualism" is the path to its future. In this region, that is no small request. The rugged individualism of which he speaks was always particularly noticeable on the American frontier, the result of a fairly potent kind of natural selection. Because the frontier was, almost by definition, a hard place to live, people did not venture lightly into it (or if they did, they did not lightly stay). Only those who were the most strongly motivated remained, and they, very often, were the ones who most deeply resented any restrictions on their individual freedom. The frontier, then, "selected" people who were willing to accept a substantial amount of hardship for the sake of being left alone. This dynamic intensified as the frontier moved into more and more forbidding territory. The harder the country, the more fiercely it selects its inhabitants, simply because it repels all those not willing to pay the price. Rugged country, then, has always selected more than its share of rugged individualists. Because the high headwaters has never stopped being hard country, it has continued to be home to a great variety of determined individualists.

But other features of the landscape also brought into the country other strains of American life. As Stegner notes, the West was never totally opened to settlement. Vast stretches of it were reserved to the "public domain" as national forests or grazing lands, while smaller tracts became national parks and wilderness areas. With this substantial reservation of federal land came a bureaucratic presence that often conflicts sharply with the rugged individualism which rooted so naturally in this soil. In fact, bureaucracy and its procedures and regulations have come into the country, not only because there was uninhabited public land to be managed, but also because of what inhabiting the land came to mean to many people. Many who came, especially in later years, began to see unfettered individualism as the greatest threat to the land and the way of life which had attracted them in the first place. These people tended to turn to regulations (and bureaucracies) to preserve the possibility of a good life in hard country. Local zoning and subdivision regulations, reclamation and major facility siting laws, stream and lakeshore protection regulations are a sample of the long list of such regulations—and of course, every regulation must have its enforcing bureaucracy.

Because the land has bred these contrasting tendencies, the politics of the region has not generally presented itself as a choice between individualism and cooperation so much as a battle between individualism and regulatory bureaucracy. Cooperation is a third, largely ignored, alternative. In this regard, the region is not atypical of the larger American political scene, although the polarization may occasionally be especially fierce here. Alasdair MacIntyre describes this essential dualism of American politics:

> On the one side there appear the self-defined protagonists of individual liberty, on the other the self-defined protagonists of planning and regulation, of the goods which are available through bureaucratic organization. But in fact what is crucial is that on which the contending parties agree, namely that there are only two alternative modes of social life open to us, one in which the free and arbitrary choices of individuals are sovereign and one in which the bureaucracy is sovereign, precisely so that it may limit the free and arbitrary choices of individuals. Given

this deep cultural agreement, it is unsurprising that the politics of modern societies oscillate between a freedom which is nothing but a lack of regulation of individual behavior and forms of collectivist control designed only to limit the anarchy of self-interest.[1]

This description of modern politics creates the suspicion that there is a missing middle. In fact, what is missing is exactly what we have already noted: that "public thing" which, in Arendt's words, "gathers us together and yet prevents our falling over each other." One of the side effects of this polarization of politics, with its missing middle, is a mutual frustration among those on either side of the struggle. Those who most forcefully promote the cause of individualism are particularly concerned about what they often refer to as the "business climate." They complain that private initiative is far too often stymied by the bureaucratic and regulatory approach. On the other hand, those who rely most heavily on that regulatory approach see themselves as promoting the "public interest," but they also very often feel that their initiatives are hopelessly stymied by the style of modern politics. Both the "public interest" and "private enterprise" tend to be blocked and frustrated by this political system. Consider just a few expressions of that frustration, beginning with a recent description of wilderness politics in Idaho:

In 1980, when [Idaho Senator Frank] Church was defeated (and died three months later), conservationists lost that powerful friend, and with him any ability to pass legislation. Afterwards, their grassroots power worked defensively, by converting John Seiberling into a passionate believer in Idaho roadless areas. Seiberling, the chair of the key House subcommittee on wilderness, insisted in 1984 on an Idaho wilderness bill too large for [Idaho Senator James] McClure to swallow. This maneuver blocked the delegation from passing anything, a little-recognized achievement for state environmentalists.

In the same years, Idaho's timber industry played wilderness politics by other means. A multi-year advertising and media campaign linked wilderness to "lockup" and job loss from mill closures. The state congressional delegation sounded the same theme for five years. As a result, the word "wilderness" has negative connotations today for a good half of Idaho's people. . . .

The result has been a deadlock. Each side has been able to block the other's initiatives.[2]

Former Governor William Janklow of South Dakota speaks in very similar terms of water politics on the Missouri. Here is how Janklow describes the suits and countersuits which South Dakota and the states downstream from it have filed over a proposed diversion of Oahe Reservoir water by a coal slurry pipeline company: "[W]e can make it difficult for them and they can make it difficult for us, and the citizens of every single state in the basin are going to be the losers. . . .The point that I'm making is anybody can wreck anything in America. Nowadays it's easy. When we couldn't do it with human ingenuity, we passed laws that make it easier for all of us to stop other people from progressing.[3]

When Janklow says that "anybody can wreck anything in America," he is expressing a frustration which arises not only over western issues like wilderness and water. John W. Gardner, a former secretary of health, education, and welfare, sees exactly the same element in urban politics:

How many times have we seen a major American city struggling with devastating problems while every possible solution is blocked by one or another powerful union or commercial or political interest? Each has achieved veto power over a piece of any possible solution, and no one has the power to solve the problem. Thus, in an oddly self-destructive conflict, the parts wage war against the whole. And the conflict will destroy us unless we get hold of it.[4]

When he asked why Americans seem to have so much difficulty in solving economic and fiscal problems, Lester Thurow reached the same conclusion: "Basically we have created the world described in Robert Ardrey's *The Territorial Imperative*. To beat an animal of the same species on his home turf, the invader must be twice as strong as the defender. But no majority is twice as strong as the minority opposing it. Therefore we each veto the other's initiatives, but none of us has the ability to create successful initiatives ourselves." [5]

All of these people who speak of our ability to block one another's initiatives are describing precisely a situation which occurs more and more frequently wherever people attempt to do something about their communities. They are describing a worsening failure of public life. To bring this failure into sharper focus, consider just a few very typical examples of local efforts at economic or community development. These examples are drawn from a few counties in Western Montana, but similar ones could be listed for almost any locality.

• A local economic development corporation is formed in Missoula, Montana, and begins to recruit businesses to locate in the community. The first live prospect is not acceptable to certain citizen-based groups, who successfully oppose the recruiting. The community ends up with no new jobs and with deep resentment on all sides, making future efforts at consensus approaches to development even less likely to succeed.

• Air pollution, much of it from residential wood burning, is making this same community less liveable and less attractive as a place to do business. Proposed wood burning regulations are opposed as an unwarranted bureaucratic intrusion into private affairs. The regulations which are finally adopted receive grudging compliance at best. No one has the will to address other components of the air pollution problem, fearing further polarization.

• Missoula needs more multifamily housing, but most proposed projects are blocked by groups fearing the deterioration of their neighborhoods. City council members and planning office staff often join forces with the neighborhood groups to stall projects. Homebuilders and developers, frustrated by the recurrence of this pattern, join the chorus of those who proclaim publicly that the community is "antibusiness."

• A new county-wide comprehensive land use plan is proposed, in part to provide a framework within which business expansion can occur in an orderly way. But the plan is successfully opposed by factions which, for various reasons, have become frustrated with government intrusion.

• In neighboring Ravalli County, citizens raised money many years ago by selling themselves stock and then used the proceeds for investment in small local businesses. This has worked well, and now they would like to sell more stock for the same purpose. But security regulations are so onerous that they end up not doing anything.

• Alberton, a small town in Mineral County, is planning a summer festival to attract some visitors and dollars to the community. Their feature event is to be a "trace race," with mountain bikes, kayaks, and hang gliders. The response is very positive until someone raises the possibility of a lawsuit. The trace race is shelved.

In all of these cases, a community or economic development initiative was blocked. Two common threads running through all of these examples, and the thousands more that could be gathered from other communities throughout the country, are, first, their less-than-zero-sum character, and, second, the fact that the particular instances of blocked initiative have cumulative effects. In each instance, the community ends up with a less satisfactory solution (fewer jobs, more air pollution, a lesser housing stock, a less exciting festival) than *any* of the residents would have chosen. As the residents learn by repeated experience that any major initiative is likely to create such negative results, the willingness to try anything new is steadily diminished.

The frequently expressed concerns about a community's or a state's "business climate" take on a different cast when viewed from this perspective. Part of what the "prodevelopment" advocates are expressing when they complain about the business climate is the feeling that enterprise is not rewarded, that new initiatives have too much trouble getting under way. Those who complain about the business climate believe that it is particularly business enterprises which face this difficulty. But in fact, the problem extends to almost any kind of enterprise or initiative. Cleaning up the air, or land use planning—even recreation—are not exempt from the tendency of our society to block new initiatives. We do have a "climate" problem, but it is not just a business climate problem. Both private enterprise and the public interest are thwarted and frustrated by this demolition derby in which the first rule seems to be, as Governor Janklow says, that "anyone can wreck anything."

How did this state of affairs come to pass? Two terms help to explain the situation. The first is Lester Thurow's reference to territoriality. The second is the term we have been struggling with from the beginning: the word *public*.

Thurow argues that the contestants in these situations act territorially, and that when a group is protecting its turf, it fights more fiercely and effectively, requiring the opponent to be stronger than most opponents in most of these struggles ever are. The result is that I may block your initiative this time, but the odds are that you will block mine tomorrow. I would argue that every one of the examples of blocked initiative listed above—from the comprehensive plan to the trace race—is covered by Thurow's analysis. In some instances, this requires giving the term *territoriality* a certain metaphorical latitude, but in other cases it can be applied quite literally. To see how this blocking of initiative actually happens, let us take a closer look at two of the examples.

A few years ago, in my home town of Missoula, Montana, a group of businessmen and bankers formed a new economic development corporation, which they named "Missoula Jobs, Inc." The group raised some money, hired a director, and began trying to entice businesses to locate in Missoula. Eventually they came within range of persuading a defense contractor to open a plant here. When word got out about which firm was being wooed, various citizen groups began gathering information about the company. They found that this contractor was an occasional supplier of nuclear weapon components. Missoula Jobs assured these concerned groups that no such components were meant to be produced in Missoula. But by then the lines were drawn. Not only the company's nuclear involvement, but also the secrecy of Missoula Jobs in its recruiting attempts became an issue. The debate was waged in terms of jobs *vs.* nuclear war or of prosperity *vs.* open dealings in public affairs. As the debate heated up, the contractor informed Missoula Jobs that it was no longer considering Missoula as a site for a plant. Before long, Missoula Jobs itself became defunct, in part because of this incident. Bitterness, frustration, and mistrust reigned among all the concerned factions. The question of whether or not Missoula was presenting an "antibusiness" face to the world became an issue in almost every local political campaign. Power shifted back and forth from one side to the other as various public issues, from land use planning to tax policy, drew more and more constituencies into the debate about Missoula's "business climate."

This is exactly the kind of behavior which Thurow says leads to deadlock over so many issues of economic development. The citizen groups which opposed the recruiting of the defense contractor probably represented a minority of the people in Missoula, but if so, they were a minority with an unusual level of commitment to the place and the way of life which they saw as theirs. This minority did act territorially, and it managed to block the Missoula Jobs initiative.

A year or two later, many of the same people who had opposed the industrial recruiting of Missoula Jobs found themselves involved in an effort to guard and secure some of what they believed was important about the place and its way of life, by getting the county to update its comprehensive land use plan. Now they were the ones who found themselves opposed by a dogged minority of rural residents who saw the draft plan as an unwarranted infringement of their private property rights. Defending their territory, these rural residents circulated petitions to have various rural communities secede from the county if the plan was adopted. In the end, the county commissioners shelved the draft comprehensive plan.

The concept of territoriality explains part of what happened in each of these instances. But to gain a fuller understanding, we need to examine the way our society makes decisions in cases like this. In particular, we have to examine the role of "public hearings." When Missoula Jobs began its decline, a special commission was established to explore the problems which had arisen and to recommend changes. The commission held a series of public hearings in preparation for making its recommendations. The planning board, too, held public hearings on the draft revision of the comprehensive plan. These are precisely the situations in which our society, as a matter of course, resorts to public hearings. This is our chosen way of involving the public in making public decisions. But there is also another, perhaps more accurate way of seeing our use of public hearings. Next to the courtroom, the public hearing room is our society's favorite arena for the blocking of one another's initiatives. It is worthwhile, therefore, to reflect for a moment on what happens at the typical public hearing.

The draft comprehensive plan was countywide in scope, and it roused an astonishing breadth and depth of ire from the rural reaches of the county. That anger poured forth at the public hearing held to review the draft plan. The proposal was labeled as communism; it was trilateralism; it was (worst of all) urban arrogance. Those who had traveled in to town to make these points, with unmistakable depth of feeling, actually encountered a touch of urban civility on that particular evening: they were allowed to testify first so that they could drive back to their homes in the country at a decent hour. So when the urban advocates of planning finally got their turn to testify, their rural neighbors were not there to hear them. But they would not likely have heard them even if they had been there—not in the sense of hearing and understanding the genuine human motivations which brought the draft plan's supporters out to city hall that night. In that deeper sense of "hearing," the urban residents who waited their turn during the early evening were not noticeably doing much hearing either. With heads shaking and eyeballs rolling, they greeted the testimony of the rural residents with disdain and contempt rather than any effort to hear the message behind their words.

In fact, out of everything that happens at a public hearing—the speaking, the emoting, the efforts to persuade the decision maker, the presentation of facts—the one element that is almost totally lacking is anything that might be characterized as "public hearing." A visitor from another planet might reasonably expect that at a public hearing there would be a public, not only speaking to itself but also hearing itself. Public hearing, in this sense, would be part of an honest conversation which the public holds with itself. But that almost never happens.

This paradox results from the role which the public hearing plays in our legal framework. Public hearings are one of the ways that we fulfill the guarantee of due process contained in both the Fifth and the Fourteenth amendments to the U.S. Constitution. There are two key components to our legal definition of due process: "notice" and "the opportunity to be heard." When we say that citizens are entitled to due process, we mean that no public entity may infringe any person's right to life, liberty, or property without giving that person notice of the intended action and an opportunity to be heard in response to it. The public hearing provides this opportunity to be heard.

But to be heard by whom? By those with the responsibility for making the ultimate decision. Public decision makers are thus constitutionally encumbered by the responsibility to hear. But the duty to hear does not extend beyond the decision maker: those who testify are not encumbered by any such responsibility. Their role, in our system, is to make the strongest possible case for their particular interests. The decision maker will then sort out, balance, or broker those interests and dispose of the case accordingly. Here is how the conservative political theorist George Will describes the process and its implicit definition of a "good society": "A good society is remarkably independent of individuals' willing the social good. A good society is a lumpy stew of individuals and groups, each with its own inherent "principle of motion." This stew stirs itself, and in the fullness of time, out comes a creamy puree called "the public interest." This is the Cuisinart theory of justice. The endless maelstrom of individuals' pursuing private goods produces, magically, the public good."[6]

Will deplores the fact that, in this model, none of the individual participants has responsibility for "willing the social good." They are not expected to do any public willing, and by the same token, they are not expected to do any public hearing. So it is that "public hearings" are curiously devoid of that very quality which their name might seem to imply.

But of course, this is simply a fulfillment of the Madisonian scheme of government. When Madison and the Federalists decided that it was unsafe to rely upon "civic virtue" to create the public interest, they fell back upon their "policy of supplying by opposite and rival interests, the defect of better motives." The modern "public hearing," at which there is no public hearing, is one unavoidable result of implementing Madison's philosophy.

Michael Sandel captures the essence of this situation in the phrase "the procedural republic and the unencumbered self."[7] The procedural republic is the natural outgrowth of the kind of politics which the Federalists embraced. Sandel and other political theorists refer to this view of politics as "liberalism," but it is important to understand that when the word *liberal* is used in this context, it has a much broader sweep than we usually give it today. The core of classical liberal doctrine is a belief in the autonomy of the individual and a defense of individual rights. This root form of liberalism is as much a part of the creed of economic conservatives as of social liberals. These two branches of liberalism often find themselves testifying against each other at public hearings, or opposing each other at elections, so we tend to think of them in terms of how they differ from one another. But as MacIntyre says, "what is crucial is that on which the contending parties agree." Sandel makes much the same point. He begins by acknowledging that economic conservatives and social liberals often appear to have nothing in common: "But whether egalitarian or libertarian, rights-based liberalism begins with the claim that we are separate, individual persons, each with our own aims, interests, and conceptions of the good; it seeks a framework of rights that will enable us to realize our capacity as free moral agents, consistent with a similar liberty in others."[8]

This "framework of rights" is the procedural republic. It is procedural, first, in the sense that it is not substantive. Sandel argues that a substantive republic might "affirm a preferred way of life or conception of the good."[9] But liberalism rests, finally, upon the assumption that only the individual is in a position to choose his or her own conception of the good. The public has no role in "affirming a preferred way of life." Roberto Mangabeira Unger, one of the formulators of Critical Legal Theory, makes this point in his exhaustive critique of Western liberalism:

> Ends are viewed by liberal theory as individual in the sense that they are always the objectives of particular individuals. . . . The political doctrine of liberalism does not acknowledge communal values. To recognize their existence, it would be necessary to begin with a vision of the basic circumstances of social life that took groups rather than individuals as the intelligible and primary units of social life. The individuality of values is the very basis of personal identity in liberal thought, a basis the communal conception of value destroys.[10]

The role of public institutions within this "procedural republic" is not to choose or impose the good, but only to provide a "framework of rights that will enable us to realize our capacity as free moral agents." The pro-choice feminist and the *laissez-faire* entrepreneur are both securely rooted in this tradition. Neither wants the public to impose on them a particular conception of the good; both ask of the public realm only that it uphold their individual rights (the right to privacy, the right to property) against infringement by other individuals, or by the government itself.

This republic, which these different kinds of liberals have united to build, is procedural, not only because it is not substantive, but also because of the emphasis which it must inevitably place upon procedural mechanisms. The "separate, individual persons" who oppose a substantive republic have to have some means of dealing with one another when their rights (or their perceptions of their rights) come into conflict. One option would be for the parties to deal with the conflict directly. But the Anglo-Saxon legal tradition decided long ago that such "self-help" was too socially destabilizing. The option that was chosen instead, as Unger argues, was the system which we now take for granted, a system of rules and concepts of rights to regulate the interaction of individuals:

> The need for rules arises from the undying enmity and the demands of collaboration that mark social life. Because there are no conceptions of the good that stand above the conflict and impose limits on it, artificial limits must be created. Otherwise, the natural hostility men have for one another will run its course relentlessly to the prejudice of their interdependence. . . . [A]ny sharing of common values will . . . be insufficient to keep the peace. . . . Peace must therefore be established by rules.[11]

The option which was chosen, then, was to place between the individuals in conflict, not a substantive choosing of a common good, but a *process* for weighing, balancing, and upholding rights. This process, which was every citizen's due, came to be known as "due process" and came to be identified principally with two procedural rights: notice, and the opportunity to be heard.

It is important to be very clear about what this process replaces—namely, direct dealings between parties in conflict. We have already seen, in the typical public hearing, some of the consequences of this act of replacement. The parties in conflict at a hearing are not encumbered by any responsibility for hearing each other, for responding to each other, for coming to an agreement about what should be done. They have given over that responsibility to "the process." Thus it is that we who inhabit the "procedural republic" find ourselves to be remarkably "unencumbered selves," in Sandel's terms. But in the process, we have also brought about the successive, mutual blocking of one another's initiatives which has so clouded the climate of enterprise, while at the same time frustrating the public interest.

Consider the example mentioned earlier of the citizens of the Bitter Root Valley—the people who wanted to sell themselves stock in order to raise some money for investment in local businesses. They had done just that many years earlier and had managed to make some good investments and add some jobs to their local economy. But now, when they decided to issue more stock, they found that the securities regulations were almost insurmountable for an enterprise of their size. Not only did they have to meet the requirements of federal and state securities laws, but they also faced the obstacles of the Investment Company Act of 1940—a stringent set of reporting requirements governing any "investment company" which by the sale of stock raises money to be invested in the securities of other companies. The people of the Bitter Root understood the motivation of the 1940 act—to protect unwary investors against exploitation by less than scrupulous individuals seeking to raise a pool of venture capital. But that was not what was happening in the Bitter Root Valley.

These were neighbors trying to raise money from within the community to help capital-short but otherwise promising local businesses get started or expand. What they were finding, to their immense frustration, was that they were not going to be allowed to treat each other like neighbors. They were going to have to act as if they were strangers to one another—as if they were isolated selves, unencumbered by any sense of responsibility to one another. Those were the kinds of people for whom the Investment Company Act of 1940 had been written, and the people of the Bitter Root were being forced into that mold whether it fit them or not.

Various exemptions are possible under the 1940 act, but none of them seemed to fit the situation in the Bitter Root. People started joking about seeking a "good guy" exemption—in effect, telling the Securities and Exchange Commission, "We're just plain folks, and we don't really need to be protected against each other in this way, so would you please just let us take our chances with ourselves?" To date, however, they have not succeeded in obtaining such an exemption. What they began to be told, instead, was that they should simply have gone ahead and sold their stock and not told anyone about it, and they would undoubtedly have escaped bureaucratic notice. Not only are they not allowed to be neighborly; they are subtly encouraged to be dishonest.

The Bitter Root is a spectacular valley, rimmed by jutting peaks which enfold the smaller creeks feeding the Bitter Root River. The canyons from which those creeks emerge have for decades drawn people whose urge to independence far outweighs their desire for ease and comfort. Four-wheel drives are a must in those canyons, and their bumpers declare the rugged individualism of their owners with raw belligerence. "This vehicle insured by Smith and Wesson," one bumper asserts. "I'm pro-choice, and I vote," shouts another. Meeting each other on the narrow canyon road, the drivers of the two vehicles will invariably wave to each other. If Smith and Wesson got stuck in a snowbank, Pro-Choice would stop and winch him out. Neither of these individualists sees anything of him- or herself in the patent wrongheadedness of the other's ideology. Neither is aware of how their unrestrained individualism has produced procedural referees like the Investment Company Act of 1940. Both would buy stock in the Bitter Root Valley Development Corporation, if it were allowed to sell stock.

The Bitter Root widens its horizons briefly as it joins the Clark Fork in the Missoula Valley. But shortly the Clark Fork finds itself in even more rugged terrain as it assaults the Rockies again in Mineral County. Here, the Alberton Gorge drowns rafters with deadly regularity. The people of Alberton know that these mountains are full of brave souls who never tire of testing themselves against this terrain. So they plan an event to see who is best, to have some fun, and to bring some money into town. They will sponsor a "trace race"—a relay race with the first leg in kayaks through the rapids of the gorge; the second on mountain bikes up rough, steep forest trails to the top of a mountain; and the third down the mountain again, riding the narrow valley's updrafts strapped to the colorful but flimsy wings of a hang glider.

The event fits the country's terrain perfectly, which is why it also suits so well the inhabitants of this and surrounding valleys. It is a certain success. But it cannot be done, because someone might hit a rock or miss an updraft and sue the town for injuries, for pain and suffering, and perhaps for punitive damages. There are more than enough contestants who would gladly sign a waiver promising not to sue no matter what happens, but no one believes that such a waiver would stop an enterprising lawyer. Like the people upriver in the Bitter Root, the folks in Alberton learn that, in the procedural republic, we are protected against each other whether we want to be or not. We cannot any longer take responsibility for our actions, directly and face-to-face. And because we cannot take responsibility for our actions, our range of activity is narrowed. What we can accomplish together is limited in ways that frustrate us deeply. We begin to growl at each other about our "business climate," but what is wrong goes much deeper than that.

In the examples we have been considering (the investment company and the trace race), the problem seems to come from outside: the local residents cannot assume the desired level of responsibility because of a federal law or because of how a state court may construe a signed waiver. Even if the local people recognized that they embrace the very individualism which undergirds these outside influences, they would still feel powerless to do anything about the situation. But there are also many instances where we, having chosen to be "unencumbered selves," have much more directly brought ourselves to a standstill. In those cases, it is more clearly within our power to do something about the situation.

I am referring here especially to those cases in which we choose to use public hearings to elicit public involvement in the making of decisions. We have already discussed how public hearings invite people to assume an unencumbered stance—to shed any responsibility for the decision or for hearing or responding to one another.

What is less apparent is that here, just as with the Investment Company Act, the intervening procedure, by discouraging people from taking face-to-face responsibility, actually diminishes their ability to get anything done.

A recent event in Wyoming helps, by its very extremity, to put the problem in perspective. Here is how the *High Country News* reported the story:

> In an unprecedented move last month, Bridger-Teton National Forest officials scrapped a Dubois, Wyo., hearing to obtain comments on the forest's draft plan. . . .
> Forest Supervisor Brian Stout said a "carnival atmosphere" promoted by Louisiana-Pacific employees and fear of violence prompted him to cancel the . . . meeting. . . .
> "This whole B-T planning process has been drawn out and negative," [a sawmill spokesman] said. "People came up with some neat ideas to change that atmosphere, such as writing their comments on two-by-fours and wheeling them in. They wanted to have some fun." [12]

There is something refreshingly honest about this approach. People rarely bring actual wooden two-by-fours to a public hearing, but both the arguments they bring and the way they wield them are merely conceptual versions of what in Dubois promised to develop into the real thing. We do not generally understand that this kind of behavior is a natural outgrowth of the narrowness of our politics, but it is. More precisely, such behavior results from our studied insistence that values are a purely private matter. As Unger says, "The political doctrine of liberalism does not acknowledge communal values. . . . The individuality of values is the very basis of personal identity in liberal thought, a basis the communal conception of value destroys." [13]

Clearly, there are values at stake over something like how to manage a national forest for the next several decades. But if those values are treated as being purely private, then the debate has an inherent tendency to move precisely in the direction of the break-down which occurred in Dubois. If values are entirely private, then there is no objective way of choosing among them. In this sense, we treat values very differently from what we call facts, as Alasdair MacIntyre explains:

> Factual judgments are true or false; and in the realm of fact there are rational criteria by means of which we may secure agreement as to what is true and what is false. But moral judgments, being expressions of attitude or feeling, are neither true nor false; and agreement in moral judgment is not to be secured by any rational method, for there are none. It is to be secured, if at all, by producing certain non-rational effects on the emotions or attitudes of those who disagree with one.[14]

This business of "producing non-rational effects on . . . emotions or attitudes" has become an increasingly important feature of what we call public life. Under a "public philosophy" which makes all values private, the two-by-fours which the Dubois sawyers were going to bring to the "public hearing" are a fairly predictable way of "producing certain non-rational effects on the emotions or attitudes of those who disagree with one." Of course, we cannot allow ourselves to use real two-by-fours very often, which means that we must work very hard to pretend that public hearings are a matter of rational discourse. But the pretense creates a terrific strain on those who participate in such "public discourse." We have to pretend that public decisions are based on objective, rational criteria, when in fact they are very often based upon values. MacIntyre describes this tension in terms of what he calls the "incommensurability" between what we pretend is happening (reason) and what is really happening (two-by-fours).

> [T]he moral idiom employed can at best provide a semblance of rationality for the modern political process, but not its reality. The mock rationality of the debate conceals the arbitrariness of the will and power at work in its resolution.

It is easy to understand why *protest* becomes a distinctive moral feature of the modern age and why *indignation* is a predominant modern emotion. . . . The self-assertive shrillness of protest arises because the facts of incommensurability ensure that protestors can never win an *argument*; the indignant self-righteousness of protestors arises because the facts of incommensurability ensure equally that the protestors can never lose an argument either.[15]

This shrillness and indignation, which is so familiar to all of us, is a symptom that something is profoundly wrong with the way we make "public" decisions. The successive blocking of one another's initiatives is another symptom. A third is the ever more frequent withdrawal of people from all public involvement—either because they are frustrated with the pattern of blocked initiative or because they don't like shrillness and indignation, in themselves or in others.

If the total privatization of values is at or near the root of this problem, then some conception of shared or communal values must be part of the solution. We began this discussion of modern stalemate, protest, and alienation by using the term *territoriality* in both a literal and a figurative sense. We continued the exploration of the demise of public life by examining how oddly the word *public* operates in a phrase like "public hearing." In turning to the idea of shared values, we will move from "territoriality" to "common ground." This phrase, too, will be used literally as well as metaphorically. And the word *public* will be taken out of its unreal context in phrases like "public hearing" and replaced, at least experimentally, within its "re*public*an" context.

Notes

1. Alasdair MacIntyre, *After Virtue*, pp. 34–35.
2. Pat Ford, "Idaho Watershed," *Northern Lights Magazine* 2, no. 5:18–19.
3. William Janklow, "High Noon in the Missouri River Basin," in *Boundaries Carved in Water*, The Missouri River Brief Series, No. 4.
4. John Gardner, speach delivered to the Humphrey Institute, April 3, 1980.
5. Lester C. Thurow, *The Zero-Sum Society*, p. 11.

6. George F. Will, *Statecraft as Soulcraft*, p. 35.
7. Michael J. Sandel, "The Procedural Republic and the Unencumbered Self," *Political Theory* 12 (February, 1984):81–96.
8. Michael J. Sandel, "Morality and the Liberal Ideal," *New Republic*, May, 1984, p. 16.
9. Ibid.
10. Roberto Mangabeira Unger, *Knowledge and Politics*, p. 76.
11. Ibid., p. 68.
12. *High Country News*, Vol. 19, No. 5 (March 16, 1987), p. 4.
13. Roberto Mangabeira Unger, *Knowledge and Politics*, p. 76.
14. Alasdair MacIntyre, *After Virtue*, p. 12.
15. Ibid., p. 71.

CHAPTER SIX

Barn Raising

In many instances in which public undertakings or community development initiatives are blocked, there is a latent public consensus that would be more satisfying to most of the participants than what finally emerges. But in fact this consensus rarely sees the light of day. Another way to say this is that in most of these cases there is more common ground, and higher common ground, than the people involved ever succeed in discovering. The common ground is there (just as it was in the stock sale or the trace race), but our prevailing way of doing things blocks us from realizing it. Our failure to realize is twofold: we do not recognize the common ground (a failure to realize its existence), and we do not make it a reality (a failure to realize its potential). This twofold failure leaves our communities poorer than they need to be.

What is it that could block us from realizing common ground? To a certain extent it is a problem of language—of how we speak publicly. This is one of the major problems identified by Robert Bellah and his coauthors in their stimulating examination of American public life, *Habits of the Heart*. In preparation for writing the book, the five authors interviewed over two hundred Americans from various walks of life, attempting to discover how these people thought about or became involved in public life. Of all the themes that emerged, the one that most consistently caught the attention of the authors was the way that people used language which portrayed them as being more isolated, more cut off from the world, than their stories showed them in fact to be. When they talked about what they valued, for example, they would consistently speak as if they had chosen those values entirely on their own, or as if they could choose others at a moment's notice, whereas their stories made it clear that the values were deeply rooted in their backgrounds, their associations, the way they lived. Or they would speak of themselves as being motivated by purely selfish considerations, when it was perfectly obvious that in their family or professional lives they were deeply committed to the common good and derived substantial satisfaction from improving the lives of other people. The consistent appearance of this incongruity became a central concern to the authors. Here are two of their ways of summarizing what they saw in the people they interviewed:

> They are responsible and, in many ways, admirable adults. Yet when each of them uses the moral discourse they share, what we call the first language of individualism, they have difficulty articulating the richness of their commitments. In the language they use, their lives sound more isolated and arbitrary than, as we have observed them, they actually are. . . .
>
> We want to make it clear that we are not saying that the people to whom we talked have empty selves. Most of them are serious, engaged, deeply involved in the world. But insofar as they are limited to a language of radical individual autonomy, as many of them are, they cannot think about themselves or others except as arbitrary centers of volition. They cannot express the fullness of being that is actually theirs.[1]

If these findings are even partially true, they would have far-reaching implications for the way we do public business. My own experience with public life persuades me that the findings are quite accurate, and that we live with their implications all the time. The most costly of those implications involves our difficulty in articulating, staking out, and building on common ground. Our story is really very much like that of the blind men and the elephant. Unable to come to a common articulation of what we are touching, we are chronically unable to benefit from its existence. To the extent that our language of individualism keeps us from naming and building upon what we have in common, we are impoverished, not only in language, but in many other ways as well.

I had a sense of this impoverishment the night that I sat in the Missoula City Council chambers and listened to the testimony on the draft comprehensive land use plan. The rural residents spoke passionately of their property rights and of their undying opposition to the urban arrogance which would presume to limit those rights in any way. The city dwellers who supported the plan spoke just as passionately of the quality of life which was so important to them and of the need they felt for some regulations to protect that quality of life against the developments which threatened it. What I did not hear was any sense of how these people's fates were woven together, how the good life that they each wanted depended upon the others being secured in a different but equally good life. It seemed to me likely that if one were to ask most of the people from outside Missoula why they lived where they did, and if they could be persuaded to speak honestly, they would talk not only about living on some particular piece of land in the country but also about living within driving distance of a town like Missoula. Missoula, in other words, is part of the place they had chosen to live—not an accidental, but an integral part. And the same would be true of the Missoulians: part of the quality of their lives depends upon their living surrounded by rural land and rural living. They have a stake in that rural life; they have a stake in its being a good life.

I heard, that evening, almost no expression of that mutual stake in the shape of one another's lives. In this sense, then, it is certainly true that, when people testify at a public hearing, "their lives sound more isolated and arbitrary than . . . they actually are." [2] People in this situation do not speak of what they have in common, or of how the common good might be guarded and enhanced. What they speak of is how a proposed initiative (in this case the land use plan) either enhances or threatens their individual rights. They speak in terms of the ideologies most conducive to their particular rights, and they leave the decision makers to choose between those opposing ideologies. Whichever side the decision makers opt for, the losing parties will either appeal to a higher decision maker or begin building political coalitions to reverse the dangerous trend which they see in this and similar decisions. But no matter how successful their coalition building, they will never, as Thurow says, be strong enough to ensure the adoption of their own initiatives. What they will ensure is the effort to build a majority coalition on the other side. So in most localities on most issues, the political pendulum is pushed back and forth endlessly, but the higher public good which everyone feels must be there never emerges.

In the example of the comprehensive plan, that higher public good can be spoken of, both figuratively and literally, as "common ground." If we try to imagine the kind of thinking which would lead people, in that situation, to work for the "higher common good," we see them acknowledging to one another that they all want to live well on a certain, very definite part of the earth. If the hearing on the comprehensive plan had been a genuine "public hearing," the people from the country would have been able to *hear* how deeply the city residents are attached to this place, how they consistently pass up higher paying work elsewhere just to be in this place, how they want their children to be able to have the benefits of open space, of small-town neighborliness which means so much to them. And they, in turn, would have heard their rural neighbors speak of how important it was to them that their children have the experience of raising some animals, of chopping wood—some of those simple, subsistence practices which Jefferson found so important. If people could actually hear the ways in which their neighbors' lives and hopes are rooted in this particular part of the earth that they all call home, they might be able to begin figuring out how to go about living well together here. But the oscillation between unrestrained individualism and stifling bureaucracy never seems to come to rest on that question.

This "missing middle" which our public policy seems never to find is in fact the *res*, the "public thing" of the "republic"—the vanishing table which could "gather us together and yet prevent us from falling over each other." It is that higher common ground which we share, yet cannot find and therefore cannot occupy. When the authors of *Habits of the Heart* describe people who "sound more isolated and arbitrary than . . . they actually are," they are seeing Arendt's "seance" in which the gathering force of the "public thing" has been removed. This, they say, is what happens when people rely, as they usually do (as they nearly always do "in public"), upon their "first language of individualism." Yet the authors of *Habits of the Heart* also found, in most cases, that these same people have some access to what they call "second languages": "[I]f the language of the self-reliant individual is the first language of American moral life, the languages of tradition and commitment in communities of memory are "second languages" that most Americans know as well, and which they use when the language of the radically separate self does not seem adequate." [3]

It is well to take a deep breath in turning from this one way of speaking to the other. It takes a while to get acclimated to an entirely new linguistic (and moral) landscape. "Tradition," "commitment," "memory," "hope"—these are not familiar landmarks in the procedural republic. We are prone to doubt that the same set of people can actually use both of these languages or occupy both of these landscapes. Is it really possible that people who can be "unencumbered selves" at a public hearing can be something quite different in another setting? In fact, it is possible, and indeed quite common. The people at the comprehensive plan hearing were certainly relying there upon their "first language of individualism"—and as a result, there was precious little public hearing going on. But there is reason to believe that those same people have access to "second languages" of "tradition and commitment" that might enable them to do a better job of seeing and articulating what they have in common.

For a start, we might refer again to language like that in the preamble to Montana's constitution. It seems likely that people on both sides of that land use hearing would feel very much the same emotional response to the words, "We the people of Montana, grateful to God for the quiet beauty of our state, the grandeur of its mountains, the vastness of its rolling plains. . . ." Here is common language, describing a relationship of diverse individuals to "common ground." The language is not that of individual rights, but of shared gratitude, echoing of humility and hope. Such language is a start toward the articulation of common ground, but standing by itself, it can readily be dismissed as mere sentimentality.

We move a step further in the right direction by remembering Wallace Stegner's call upon the people of the West (the "native home of hope") to create a "society to match its scenery." Stegner's argument is that this can only be done by relying upon some other language and culture than that of "rugged individualism." In calling for a renewal of the culture of cooperation, he invokes the barn building culture of the not yet forgotten days of the frontier. He thus calls to mind precisely a "language of tradition and commitment" which Westerners as a "community of memory" can still recall. Calling that culture to mind is a natural function of centennial celebrations. We need to spend time in such celebrations, in such remembering. But this should not be merely an exercise in nostalgia. At its best, such recalling can serve the same purpose as language like that of Montana's preamble: it can help to remind us, in an active, creative way, of what we have in common. In describing the "second language of commitment," Bellah speaks of the importance of these common bonds: "We know ourselves as social selves, parents and children, members of a people, inheritors of a history and a culture that we must nurture through memory and hope. . . .In order not to forget that past, a community is involved in retelling its story, its constitutive narrative, and in so doing, it offers examples of the men and women who have embodied and exemplified the meaning of community."[4]

In this spirit, I will tell one brief story about some men and women who have helped me understand what "cooperation" might mean. Most of us could tell different versions of this same story.

By the time I was eight or nine years old, the wind that blew almost ceaselessly across the high plains of eastern Montana had taken its toll on our barn. We planned to tear down the old one and from its remnants build a new barn in the swale of a dry creek bank, high enough to avoid the torrents that roared through every year or two. It never would have occurred to us, in the early 1950s, to tackle this massive job without calling on the neighbors for help.

Since my brother and I were too young to be of much help to the builders, we spent most of the day down among the box elders on the creek bottom playing with the neighbor children. That day stands out clear in my mind, not so much for the image of the new barn rising out of the old, but for the fact that our neighbor, Albert Volbrecht, had brought his children along. We didn't exactly play with Albert's children; we listened to them tell dirty stories that would have made our mother, Lilly, frying chicken up in the house, cry with rage. What fascinated me was the fact that the little Volbrecht girl was the one in the family with the best stock of stories. Her younger brothers revered her, at least on that score, for her prowess.

Though my mother did not know the exact wording of the stories the Volbrecht girl was entertaining us with, she did know the kind of language the child used under other circumstances, and she heartily disapproved. She would have done anything in her power to deny my brother and me that part of our education. But there was nothing she could do about it. The Volbrechts had to be at the barn raising, just as they had to be there when we branded calves. They were neighbors, and that was that. Albert's presence loomed large on the scene no matter the situation. His hat was the biggest in the corral, his voice the loudest, his language the foulest, his intake of beer the most prodigious. His influence was pervasive. I saw my father drink a can of beer once after the last calf was branded. I was astonished to see him do such a thing, and so was my mother. The blame for my father's indiscretion came to rest on Albert. Like his children, Albert was too fond of off-color stories for my mother's taste. The simplest event became colorful, wild, when Albert retold it. My mother accused him of being unable to open his mouth without storying. And Albert, for his part, delighted in watching my mother squirm at his bawdy jokes.

In another time and place, Albert and Lilly would have had nothing to do with one another. But on those Montana plains, life was still harsh enough that they had no choice. Avoiding people you did not like was not an option. Everyone was needed by everyone else in one capacity or another. If Albert and Lilly could have snubbed one another, our barn might not have been built, and neither our calves nor Albert's branded. Lilly and Albert didn't like each other much better at the end of the barn raising than at the beginning. But that day, and many others like it, taught them something important. They learned, whether they liked it or not, a certain tolerance for another slant on the world, another way of going at things that needed doing. They found in themselves an unsuspected capacity to accept one another. This acceptance, I believe, broadened them beyond the boundaries of their own likes and dislikes and made these personal idiosyncrasies seem less important. In addition, they learned that they could count on one another. If Albert said he would be there with a "farmhand" attachment on his tractor to lift the roof into place, he would be there with the "farmhand." If Lilly said she would fry the chicken, she would do it whether she was in the mood that morning or not. And because Albert and Lilly and the rest of our neighbors were able to count on one another, they experienced the satisfaction of accomplishing a big, tough job by working together.

This eastern Montana of my boyhood still echoed of the frontier. From Plymouth Rock onwards, Americans on the frontier had found themselves united with their neighbors in the face of an often hostile and precarious existence. Over the generations, the lessons of cooperation wove themselves into something that can only be called political education. People who had learned by repeated experience that they could count on each other, and in doing so accomplish difficult and important tasks together, were the people who eventually formed cooperatives to bring electricity to the most remote areas or to market wheat or beef out of those areas. This way of working together was still taken for granted in my childhood. When early in the 1950s the rural electric association lines marched across the hill to our farmstead, bringing us the magic of electricity, I was oblivious to the fact that generations of Alberts and Lillys learning to work together were behind this miracle.

The point here is not nostalgia. We cannot re-create the world of the frontier, even if we thought we wanted to. But there is something to be learned from the subtle but persistent process by which frontier families learned the politics of cooperation. They learned it the way almost anything worthwhile is learned—by practice. Republican theorists have always understood that citizens do not become capable of democratic self-determination by accident. As Bellah points out, republicans from Montesquieu to Jefferson (and we might add the populists) had recognized that the character which is required for participation in face-to-face self-government can only be instilled through repeated experiences of a very specific kind. For these democratic republicans, " . . . the virtuous citizen was one who understood that personal welfare is dependent on the general welfare and could be expected to act accordingly. Forming such character requires the context of practices in which the coincidence of personal concern and the common welfare can be *experienced* [emphasis added]." [5]

From childhood, Albert and Lilly and all of their neighbors were schooled in those experiences. Because of that practical education, they could overcome many of their differences; they could recognize their need for one another and act accordingly. By contrast, the people at the comprehensive plan hearing had gone to a very different school, and they, too, acted accordingly. Their differences seemed insurmountable to them, and they seemed to see little of their mutual need for one another. The political education which had created this pessimism and isolation is exemplified by another brief story.

A group of citizens in a western town recently began making plans to initiate a major annual art and music festival. During the first summer, they wanted to hold a small one-day preview event, both to raise awareness within the community about the larger festival idea and to raise some money for the next year's festival. They settled on the idea of an old-fashioned box social, where people would be asked to bring picnic lunches, which could then be auctioned. The idea gathered momentum quickly and seemed like a nearly certain success until someone pointed out the possibility of a lawsuit. What if someone got sick from one of the lunches and filed suit? With that question, the box social was laid to rest.

How could it be that my parents and their neighbors could have box socials but we cannot? I have tried to imagine Albert suing us because my mother's fried chicken laid him up or because he got hurt in our corral. But it is truly unimagineable. He no more had that option than we had the choice of not inviting him to help with the barn because we disapproved of the way he or his kids told stories. Most of us now do have those options, and as a society, we pursue them with a vengeance. We have as little as possible to do with those whose "life-styles" make us uncomfortable. If we are injured by one of "them" (or even by one of "us"), we will not lightly shrink from a lawsuit. Short of that, we readily and regularly oppose each other at public hearings, avidly pursuing our own interests and protecting our own rights with no sense of responsibility to hear or respond to the legitimate interests of those on the "other side" or to discover common ground. More and more often, the result is deadlock—and then frustration and withdrawal from all things public. Whereas the politics of cooperation gave people a robust sense of their capacity to get big, tough jobs done together, we increasingly come to the gloomy conclusion that "anybody can wreck anything," so there is no purpose in trying anything. We have been practiced in the politics of alienation, separation, and blocked initiatives rather than in any "practices of commitment" which might "give us the strength to get up and do what needs to be done."

Yet one of the lessons of *Habits of the Heart* is that even those who testified on the Missoula comprehensive plan, even those who never got to testify on the Dubois forest plan, do have some experience with "the second languages and practices of commitment." They do not have enough of that experience to change the way they behave at a public hearing, and that is a growing problem for our society. But they do have snatches of such experience, and it is there that the possibility of reform must be sought. Here, picked almost at random, are a few examples of such "practices of commitment":

• Children in a 4-H club are taught to raise and care for animals, preparing for the competition at the county fair.

• Residents of a rural community form and maintain a volunteer fire department.

• Urban residents create a neighborhood watch program for their block.

• Other urban residents form a softball league, carrying their competition through to the fall championships.

As with instances of community deadlock, these examples can also be multiplied almost endlessly. And as with those other examples, these, too, share certain common features. Those features are essential ingredients in any revitalization of public life, either in this region or in the nation itself. But because that connection is far from obvious, it will bear some deliberate looking into.

There are two basic ingredients of practices such as those listed here or the thousands of others which might have been listed instead. It is the combination of these two ingredients which give to these practices the potential for revitalizing public life. The two elements are: 1) a central concern with value, with standards of excellence, with what is good; and 2) a rigorous objectivity. What these practices promise (and what, in fact, nothing else can provide) is the kind of experience which would enable us to identify and build upon common ground. The common ground we need to find is like a high, hidden valley which we know is there but which seems always to remain beyond our reach. This hidden valley may be called common ground because it is a place of shared values. The values are shared because they are objective; they are, in fact, public values. This is what makes this common ground valuable, but it is also what keeps it hidden from us. It is valuable because the reclaiming of a vital, effective form of public life can only happen if we can learn to say words like *value* in the same breath with words like *public* or *objective.*

But this valley of common ground remains hidden because we all inhabit a world in which values are always private, always subjective. Always, that is, except when we are engaged in practices. What barn building and violin playing, softball and steer raising all have fundamentally in common is this: all of them deal with questions of value, with what is good or excellent (a well-built barn; a well-executed double play), but they all do so in an explicitly social setting, wherein purely subjective or individualistic inclinations are flatly irrelevant, if not counterproductive. MacIntyre explains why:

> If, on starting to listen to music, I do not accept my own incapacity to judge correctly, I will never learn to hear, let alone to appreciate, Bartok's last quartets. If, on starting to play baseball, I do not accept that others know better than I when to throw a fast ball and when not, I will never learn to appreciate good pitching let alone to pitch. In the realm of practices the authority of both goods and standards operates in such a way as to rule out all subjectivist and emotivist analyses of judgment.[6]

What MacIntyre says here of baseball or Bartok may also be said of the thousands of examples of practices which people engage in, from raising steers to running a rural fire department. No one can do these things in a "practiced" way while maintaining a purely subjectivist approach to values. People who engage in these kinds of activities experience what it is to operate within a system of shared values, in which it is clearly not enough to say, "Well, those may be your values, but these are mine." Everyone who testifies at a public hearing may act on that occasion as if all values are subjective and may therefore contribute to the difficulty we have in acting upon shared values. But for most of those people, there is at least one part of their lives where they act, think, and talk very differently. Whether they are cross-country skiing or raising prize irises, they come into relationship with other people in a very particular way. "Every practice," according to MacIntyre, "requires a certain kind of relationship between those who participate in it."[7] What that relationship instills, over time, are precisely the "civic virtues"—those habits which would be necessary if people were ever to relate to each other in a truly public way. Here is how MacIntyre describes how even our homeliest practices gradually instill these civic virtues:

> We have to learn to recognize what is due to whom; we have to be prepared to take whatever self-endangering risks are demanded along the way; and we have to listen carefully to what we are told about our own inadequacies and to reply with the same carefulness for the facts. In other words we have to accept as necessary components of any practice with internal goods and standards of excellence the virtues of justice, courage and honesty.[8]

What Hannah Arendt calls the "weirdness" of our modern situation may be reduced to this: that in what we call the "public" realm, all of these virtues which might in fact enable us to be public are suddenly overshadowed. The "second language of commitment," which so many public hearing contestants speak in their softball leagues or their PTA meetings, becomes suddenly silent when these people think they are in a public setting. Instead, in that setting, they speak their "first language of individualism," with consequences which are all too familiar. The person who grew up knowing that she could not arbitrarily decide what constitutes a prize-winning steer or a good time to bunt now accepts as utterly natural the idea that what she considers a good community is "her value" and what her opponent considers a good community is "his value." What this does to the tone of "public" discourse is predictable: "From our rival conclusions we can argue back to our rival premises, but when we do arrive at our premises argument ceases and the invocation of one premise against another becomes a matter of pure assertion and counter-assertion. Hence perhaps the slightly shrill tone of so much moral debate.[9]

At the root of this difficulty, MacIntyre discovers the same feature which struck the authors of *Habits of the Heart* so forcibly: the feeling on the part of most people that, in the end, their positions (and certainly the positions of their opponents) are a result, not of reason, but of individual inclination.

> [I]f we possess no unassailable criteria, no set of compelling reasons by means of which we may convince our opponents, it follows that in the process of making up our own minds we can have made no appeal to such criteria or such reasons. If I lack any good reasons to invoke against you, it must seem that I lack any good reasons. Hence it seems that underlying my own position there must be some non-rational decision to adopt that position. Corresponding to the interminability of public argument there is at least the appearance of a disquieting private arbitrariness. It is small wonder if we become defensive and therefore shrill.[10]

We are faced, then, with a considerable paradox. While many people do receive training in civic virtues, and are therefore capable of at least a halting fluency in the "second language of commitment," the place that they are least likely to use that language is in what we call public settings. Our public discourse is couched almost entirely in the framework which MacIntyre identifies as the dichotomy of regulated versus unregulated individuality. If people think of public choices only in these terms, it is not surprising that they use in any public setting the "first language of individualism." This, then, is where people "have difficulty articulating the richness of their commitments"; this is where "their lives sound more isolated and arbitrary than . . . they actually are"; here, where the capacity to identify shared values is most acutely needed, it is most consistently lacking.[11] So what can be done about this deadly paradox? If it is true that people attain civic virtues through practices, and if it is true that many people gain such education outside the public arena, the obvious question is: "What can be done to establish practices which would teach people to act and speak in a truly public way in public?"

There is no simple answer to that question. But one part of the answer may emerge from understanding how important to practices is the concrete, the specific, the tangible. It is precisely that element of concreteness which gives to practices their capacity to present values as something objective, and therefore as something public. Again, we need to recall Arendt's table—that actual, physical thing, the *res* which makes the public (the common unity or community) possible at all. Lawrence Haworth has perhaps best understood the essential connection between the concepts of community and objectivity: "In any genuine community there are shared values: the members are united through the fact that they fix on some object as preeminently valuable. And there is a joint effort, involving all members of the community, by which they give overt expression to their mutual regard for that object."[12]

In the case of my parents and their neighbors, this matter of objectivity may be viewed on several levels. The barn itself was an "object" which, being a straightforward matter of life and death, seems to qualify as being "preeminently valuable." The barn was as real, as objective, as anything could be, but it only acquired its urgency within the context of the broader and even more compelling objectivity of the land and the weather to which it was a response. However Albert and Lilly may have differed in some of their personal values, they differed not at all in their experience of winter on the high plains. For both of them alike, the prairie winter was cold and deadly, and it absolutely required a good barn.

Strangely enough, that objective requirement of a good barn meant that they were not free to treat their values as being purely subjective. In some things they could afford to be subjective, to be sure. Albert could value beer and salty language in a way that Lilly never would. But when it came to values like reliability, perseverance, or even a certain level of conviviality, they found themselves dealing in something much more objective than we generally think of "values" as being. In fact, those people could no more do without those values than they could do without their barns, simply because they could not get the barns built without the values. The shaping of their values was as much a communal response to their place as was the building of their barns.

The kinds of values which might form the basis for a genuinely public life, then, arise out of a context which is concrete in at least two ways. It is concrete in the actual things or events—the barns, the barn dances—which the practices of cooperation produce. But it is also concrete in the actual, specific places within which those practices and that cooperation take place. Clearly, the practices which shaped the behavior and the character of frontier families did not appear out of thin air; they grew out of the one thing those people had most fundamentally in common: the effort to survive in hard country. And when the effort to survive comes to rely upon shared and repeated practices like barn raising, survival itself is transformed; it becomes inhabitation. To in*habit* a place is to dwell there in a practiced way, in a way which relies upon certain regular, trusted habits of behavior.

Our prevailing, individualistic frame of mind has led us to forget this root sense of the concept of "inhabitation." We take it for granted that the way we live in a place is a matter of individual choice (more or less constrained by bureaucratic regulations). We have largely lost the sense that our capacity to live well in a place might depend upon our ability to relate to neighbors (especially neighbors with a different life-style) on the basis of shared habits of behavior. Our loss of this sense of inhabitation is exactly parallel to our loss of the "republican" sense of what it is to be public.

In fact, no real public life is possible except among people who are engaged in the project of inhabiting a place. If there are not habituated patterns of work, play, grieving, and celebration designed to enable people to live well in a place, then those people will have at best a limited capacity for being public with one another. Conversely, where such inhabitory practices are being nurtured, the foundation for public life is also being created or maintained. This suggests a fairly intimate connection between two potent strains of contemporary American thought. One is the revival of interest in civic republicanism. The other appears frequently under the title of "bioregionalism." That word raises issues of definition which need not detain us here. (I mean specifically the challenge of defining any particular bioregion with lines on a map.) What is of particular interest in this context is the tendency of bioregionalists to identify their work by the word *re-inhabitation*. In a talk with that title, Gary Snyder evokes the connection between "coming into the country" and the habituated ways which make it possible to stay there: "Countless local ecosystem habitation styles emerged. People developed specific ways to *be* in each of those niches: plant knowledge, boats, dogs, traps, nets, fishing—the smaller animals, and smaller tools." These "habitation styles" carried with them precisely the element of objectivity which MacIntyre and Haworth emphasize. Habitation, in other words, implies right and wrong ways of doing things: "Doing things right means living as though your grandchildren would also be alive, in this land, carrying on the work we're doing right now, with deepening delight."[13]

In this talk, as elsewhere, Snyder acknowledges his debt to Wendell Berry's teachings about practiced ways of living in places. Berry makes clear to us why the concept of inhabitation is broader and deeper than "environmentalism":

> The concept of country, homeland, dwelling place becomes simplified as "the environment"—that is, what surrounds us. Once we see our place, our part of the world, as *surrounding* us, we have already made a profound division between it and ourselves. We have given up the

understanding—dropped it out of our language and so out of our thought—that we and our country create one another, depend on one another, are literally part of one another; that our land passes in and out of our bodies just as our bodies pass in and out of our land; that as we and our land are part of one another, so all who are living as neighbors here, human and plant and animal, are part of one another, and so cannot possibly flourish alone; that, therefore, our culture must be our response to our place, our culture and our place are images of each other and inseparable from each other, and so neither can be better than the other.[14]

Berry and Snyder present some of the best thinking and writing about this intimate relationship of place and culture, including, crucially, the awareness of how places, by developing practices, create culture. The civic republicans, in a sense, take up where these writers leave off. That is, they recognize the crucial role of practices, not only in the development of culture, but also in the revitalization of public life. Here is how Bellah speaks of what he calls "practices of commitment":

People growing up in communities of memory not only hear the stories that tell how the community came to be, what its hopes and fears are, and how its ideals are exemplified in outstanding men and women; they also participate in the practices—ritual, aesthetic, ethical—that define the community as a way of life. We call these "practices of commitment" for they define the patterns of loyalty and obligation that keep the community alive.[15]

There is considerable room for more mutual reinforcement of these two strains of understanding. The political philosophy of the bioregionalists tends to be vague, uncertain, often more than a little precious and utopian. A more solid, and therefore more confident understanding of how place-centered practices could transform public life would do much to make re-inhabitory politics more credible. The civic republicans are developing very valuable insights into this potentially transformative power of homely practices; what they tend to underemphasize is precisely what the bioregionalists understand so well: the essential role of place in developing those practices.

It is in what Bellah calls "communities of memory" that these "second languages and practices of commitment" have been most carefully preserved. Because of this, it has seemed appropriate to take the occasion of centennial (and bicentennial) celebrations to help us recall how cooperation could once have become such an important part of our culture. But of course there comes a time for turning from what was to what may be. If public life needs to be revitalized, if its renewal depends upon more conscious and more confident ways of drawing upon the capacity of practices to make values objective and public, if those practices acquire that power from the efforts of unlike people to live well in specific places, then we need to think about specific places, and the real people who now live in them, and try to imagine ways in which their efforts to live there might become more practiced, more inhabitory, and therefore more public.

There are two arenas within which this move toward a more inhabitory and more public life must occur if it is to sustain itself. One is the arena of economics; the other, that of politics. The final two chapters will explore the concept of re-inhabitation in those two contexts.

Notes

1. Robert N. Bellah et al., *Habits of the Heart*, pp. 20–21, 81.
2. Ibid., p. 21.
3. Ibid., p. 154.
4. Ibid., pp. 138, 153.
5. *Ibid.*, p. 254. Emphasis added.
6. Alasdair MacIntyre, *After Virtue*, p. 190.
7. Ibid., p. 191.
8. Ibid.
9. Ibid., p. 8.

10. Ibid.
11. Bellah et al., *Habits of the Heart*, pp. 20–21.
12. Lawrence Haworth, *The Good City*, p. 86.
13. From remarks given at the "Reinhabitation Conference" at North San Juan School, held under the auspices of the California Council on the Humanities, August, 1976.
14. *Ibid.*
18. Wendell Berry, *The Unsettling of America*, p. 22.
15. Bellah et al., *Habits of the Heart*, p. 154.

CHAPTER SEVEN

Reclaiming the Marketplace
(The Economics of Re-Inhabitation)

Economics is referred to as the dismal science because it deals in the inescapable limitations and hardships of human existence. If Adam and Eve had never been expelled from the Garden of Eden, there would be no economists. Economics is not the science of allocating plentiful resources; it ruminates instead on the allocation of short supplies. The species condemned to live by the sweat of its brow is the species that invents economics. But clearly there is more to the story. People do not study economics or read the words of economists in newspapers simply in order to remind themselves again of the bitter facts of scarcity and hardship. Opportunity, hope, and the possibility of the good life are endlessly sought in the face of these earthly limitations, and this seeking is no small part of what we mean by "economics." It is here, at the intersection of hardship and opportunity, that economics takes on its human significance. It is here that the economy becomes important to ordinary men and women.

But the economy is placed, or located, not only in terms of its particular way of addressing the human condition. The economy has place or locale in a more physical sense as well. The Greek root for our word *economy* was *oikos*, which meant "household." To the

Greeks, economics was the art of household management. It was the interplay of hardship and opportunity within the particular, bounded setting of a specific household which the Greeks would call "the economy."

We no longer think of the household as the locus of the economy, but we continue to assume that economies do have particular, bounded settings. For the last two centuries, the unchallenged assumption has been that the natural setting of an economy was the nation-state. America declared itself a nation in 1776, the same year that Adam Smith's *The Wealth of Nations* appeared. That book not only took for granted that nations are in fact the locus of economies; it also provided the enduring definition of "economic man" as an essentially isolated actor, making his production or consumption decisions with regard only for his own well-being. The larger good emerged, not from anyone actively willing it, but from the "invisible hand" of the market, which wove all of these isolated acts of will into a greater good.

In chapter 2 we noted the parallel between Smith's impersonal, mechanistic market and James Madison's political philosophy. Madison's view of public life substantially replaced any direct willing of a common good with a procedural framework which encouraged individuals to pursue their own ends, relying upon the impersonal machinery of government to weave these individual interests into a common good. It is not altogether surprising that the political theory which buttressed the new Constitution bore such a marked resemblance to the economic theory of *The Wealth of Nations*. The driving force behind the Constitution, with its revision of republican theory, was economic. Both the expansion of commerce on this continent, and its protection against foreign interference, seemed to require the strengthening of a central government. Adam Smith made two assumptions, and James Madison agreed with both of them: first, that strong, growing economies presuppose nation-states, and second, that they presuppose a highly impersonal, atomistic set of relationships among the people who make up those nations. America becoming a nation and America becoming an economy proved, therefore, to be one and the same story, which was and had to be, at the same time, the story of the eclipse of republicanism. Out of a confederation of small republics a nation emerged and began to grow, both economically and territorially. In time, the nation, with its muscular national economy, became a world power. In time, again, its power and ascendancy began to decline.

With the decline, with America moving overnight from being the world's largest creditor nation to being the most deeply indebted, the two-century-old assumption that nations are the natural locus of economies has suddenly come under an unaccustomed scrutiny. The challenge to this sacred assumption has arisen, simultaneously, from two very different quarters. On the one hand, there is a growing chorus of commentators who argue that American businesses cannot regain their competitiveness until they recognize that they are operating not in a national, but in a global economy. At the same time, the primacy of the national economy is challenged from below by theories which argue that entities smaller than nations are the natural locus of economies. The most trenchant argument from this school is presented by Jane Jacobs. In *Cities and the Wealth of Nations*, Jacobs challenges the entire tradition inaugurated by Adam Smith's classic work by arguing that cities, not nations, are the natural, organic economic entities. Jacobs' argument is not simply theoretical, but also practical: her interest is in what actually enables or helps economies to grow. As Jacobs puts it, "Distinctions between city economies and the potpourris we call national economies are important not only for getting a grip on realities; they are of the essence where practical attempts to re-shape economic life are concerned.[1]

The crux of Jacobs' argument is that what actually makes economies grow is import substitution—replacing goods that were once imported with goods that are produced by the economy in question. But this vital economic activity has, according to Jacobs, a very specific locus, which is not that of the nation-state: "[T]he all-important function of import-replacing or import-substitution is in real life specifically a city function, rather than something a "national economy" can be made to do." [2] While Jacobs considers cities to be the most vital and important actors in economic matters, it is not cities alone, but what she calls "cities and their regions," or simply "city regions," which constitute economies. Thus, while Jacobs would presumably have some difficulty with a term like "a rural economy" (since an economy presupposes a city), she would also have difficulty with the idea of a purely "urban economy" (since a city must have a hinterland region in order to be an active economy). This relationship of city and country in Jacobs' theory is especially provocative against the background of Jefferson's and Hegel's conflicting views of the roles of rural and urban development. That subject will be addressed in the next chapter. For now, my main interest in Jacobs' analysis is her argument that import substitution is the main engine of real, sustainable economic development.

Jacobs' entire argument is summed up in these two sentences: "Economic life develops by grace of innovating; it expands by grace of import-replacing. These two master economic processes are closely related, both being functions of city economies." [3]

There are two features of this emphasis upon import substitution which deserve special notice. One is that it is fundamentally, indeed aggressively, entrepreneurial in its orientation. This means, among other things, that it presumes a very active role for the "free market" as an indispensable tool for building strong economies. But in addition to being entrepreneurial, this view of economic activity is also strikingly place-centered. What this means is that the market within which a vital entrepreneurship operates is not simply an abstract market; it is, in a deep sense, a market*place*.

Our age tends to use the terms *market* and *marketplace* interchangeably, but in fact, no matter which term we use, we ascribe to the market no place at all, in the actual, physical, concrete sense of the word. When we acclaim the "magic of the marketplace," or decry the shortcomings of the marketplace, we actually have no concept of place in mind; we mean the "market" in an explicitly footloose, generalized, and universal sense. It was precisely within this kind of market that Adam Smith's "invisible hand" was able to operate so effectively. But when we begin to emphasize something like import substitution, we in effect re-place the market within a specific location. It makes no sense to speak of import substitution in the abstract; it only makes sense if we are talking about a specific place producing for itself what it had previously imported from some other place. To advocate import substitution as a tool for building an economy is to say, "These specific goods should be produced, not just for *the* market, but for *this* market, in *this* place."

Jacobs' emphasis on import substitution is of interest not only because of whatever theoretical cogency it may have, but also because so many local communities are, in various ways, acting as if some such theory were true. Beyond doubt, many of these same communities also act as if other, totally inconsistent theories were equally true. My point here is not that import substitution is embraced with any consistency, but only that, in the current fascination with economic development, it is one of the theories which is more and more frequently embraced by real communities in specific locations. However dimly these communities may understand the implications of the theory they are toying with, the partial embrace by a large number of localities of the concept of import substitution has the potential to transform very substantially the economic life of this country.

It is the way in which the theory of import substitution responds to the specific character of a particular location that gives it this transformative power. Almost without exception, any serious move toward import substitution by a local economic development organization goes hand in hand with an effort to identify and describe the characteristics of that locality which set it apart and give it a distinct identity. This exercise in community self-awareness is crucial to any concerted effort at import substitution. Import replacement depends upon a particularly close match between a place and its people; it depends upon a working understanding of what the place can feasibly produce which, at the same time, many of the residents want or need. These are economic considerations in the most classical sense; they seek that particular intersection of limitation and possibility within which economies are born. But when a locality engages in these ruminations, it necessarily (although seldom explicitly) challenges the presumption that the nation is the most relevant economic entity. Getting serious about import replacement means taking the locality seriously as the "household" within which limitations and possibilities may yield a strong and stable economy. To elucidate this point, I will turn again to my own home community in western Montana. If I use the specific example of the place I happen to inhabit, it is not at all because I think there is anything special about its situation, but because the revitalization of public and economic life must be accomplished in the context of specific places, and this happens to be the one I know best. But there are few local settings to which the same principles could not be applied.

Missoula, Montana, is located in a broad mountain valley over which cold wintertime air tends to hover inertly, trapping the warmer air (and whatever happens to be in it) near the valley floor. Surrounding the valley, for miles on all sides, are vast stretches of coniferous forests. Like the particular shape and location of the Missoula Valley, those forests have long defined Missoula, giving shape both to its potential and to its problems. The role of trees is testified to by the fact that Region I of the U.S. Forest Service, the Forestry Division of the Montana Department of State Lands, and many forest-related businesses are headquartered in Missoula.

But the trees have also, in various ways, run up against those wintertime air inversions. Soft wood like this makes good paper, and in the 1950s a pulp mill was constructed west (upwind) of Missoula. Its hydrogen sulfide and other airborne offerings would float into town, get trapped, get breathed, get cursed by some, and make others respond, "Well you can't eat clean air!" Time and again the plant divided the people of the valley bitterly against each other. But the trees were not only going into paper; they were also (especially after the energy shocks of the 1970s) going into people's wood stoves and fireplaces, and on into the air in forms which began to prove even more deadly than the pulp mill fumes.

Here was an example of import substitution: a home-grown energy source was being substituted for imported energy. But to make a lasting difference to a local economy, import substitution must fit the place; it must be an appropriate response to the possibilities and the limitations of the place. Given the air inversion problems of the Missoula Valley, it was not at all clear that this particular form of import substitution could work in this place. Health studies proved that Missoula children had a substantially higher incidence of pulmonary problems than children in other locations. Missoula frequently exceeded federal clean air standards. Industrial recruiting and other forms of economic development also came to be affected, either because new sources of pollution were prohibited from adding to the already illegal levels of pollution, or simply because business owners were not interested in living in a polluted setting. Finally, it got so bad that wood burning regulations came before the county commissioners and the city council, and the people divided against each other again. "You mean you're going to tell me now that I can't go into the forest and cut my own wood and take it home and burn it in my own living room fireplace? What are we here—a bunch of communists?" And so on.

It would be possible for Missoula to regulate wood burning in such a way that many people would be forced to stop burning wood altogether. From the perspective of the airshed, this may seem, at first glance, to be a good solution. But in fact what it would almost certainly mean is that these people would become more dependent upon nonlocal, nonrenewable sources of energy like electricity or natural gas. While there are certainly cases where this kind of fuel substitution is entirely appropriate, it can also be a way of shifting from one community to another both problems and opportunities. If air pollution in one place is replaced by depletion of a nonrenewable resource in another, is there really an improvement, or merely the postponement of a problem? Furthermore, if the substitution means that fuel which was for a time produced locally must now again be imported, the local economy will suffer a loss which may be quite substantial.

With the use of proper equipment, wood can be burned quite cleanly. If this particular community is going to pursue import substitution by replacing electricity or natural gas with wood, it is this clean-burning route which it must pursue. In fact, meeting the challenge of wood burning in a place like Missoula can actually carry import substitution to a new level of potency which would very likely never be achieved in a setting where wood burning is less problematic. To understand this, it is helpful to explore in greater detail why Jacobs argues that import substitution is "at the root of all economic expansion." [4] The primary effect of import substitution is to interrupt some of the flow of dollars outside the community. But as Jacobs describes it, any substantial substitution of imports is likely to have even more far-reaching and beneficial effects upon the local economy: "Cities that replace imports significantly replace not only finished goods, but, concurrently, many, many items of producers' goods and services. For example, first comes the local processing of fruit preserves that were formerly imported, then the production of jars or wrappings formerly imported for which there was no local market of producers until the first step had been taken." [5]

The dynamic which Jacobs ascribes to import substitution is essentially what Missoula has experienced in attempting to substitute wood, a locally produced fuel, for imported fuel. But it is precisely in response to Missoula's air pollution problem that this economic expansion has occurred. This is simply an illustration of the time-honored entrepreneurial maxim that "necessity is the mother of invention." As Missoulians have responded simultaneously to the inviting combustibility of the surrounding trees and the air-trapping contours of their valley, a number of inventions have emerged. There is now a significant handful of local businesses within Missoula's city region which are profitably engaged in manufacturing clean-burning stoves, or compressed wood pellets to burn cleanly in them, or furnace accessories to enable commercial or institutional consumers to burn these pellets. The success of each of these industries has added to the momentum of import substitution. The result has been precisely the kind of vital, dynamic, mutually reinforcing entrepreneurship which Jacobs argues is the only true engine for building economies. Here is an example, then, of how the effort to inhabit a place—to respond to things like trees and airsheds—can lead to import substitution and from there to a healthy, indigenous kind of growth in the local economy. Notice, however, that this kind of economic development is not possible without a shift in thinking which replaces the abstract, placeless notion of the market with the localized, particularized concept of a market*place*.

This leads us to the question of whether there are ways to move economies in a more place-focused direction. In other words, are real marketplaces only created by chance—by the operation of another kind of invisible hand—or is there something that public policy can do to help them emerge? To help answer this question, consider the case of two citizens' initiatives which appeared on the Montana ballot in the early 1980s. Both initiatives grew in part out of frustration with the workings of the Montana legislature. The first issue centered on regulatory control of milk production, distribution, and prices. Like many other states, Montana had long ago established a Milk Control Board with power to set standards for milk quality and cleanliness, to regulate producers and distributors, and even, eventually, to control milk prices as a means of avoiding the temptation to cut costs by relaxing hygienic standards.

In the late seventies and early eighties, a small but determined libertarian movement emerged in Montana, with one foot in the Republican party and the other in its own Libertarian party. This movement carefully picked issues to advance its cause, and it developed a very effective strategy of playing the legislature off against the citizen initiative process. Libertarians, for example, brought an income tax indexing bill to the legislature, where it narrowly failed to pass. In the next election, they used the resulting voting record against those legislators who had opposed the bill, but they also had their own candidates supporting a ballot measure to enact indexing. The initiative passed with a solid majority, and carried several candidates with a libertarian philosophy into the legislature. It was into this legislature that the libertarians introduced a bill to decontrol milk production and prices. Opposed by the dairy industry, the bill was defeated, creating again a situation in which the libertarians could use both voting records and a ballot initiative to advance their cause. The next election, then, gave Montana voters a chance to reverse the legislature again by adopting a measure to abolish the Milk Control Board.

As with income tax indexing, the proponents of this initiative expected strong consumer support, since it was indisputable that abolishing milk control would lower most retail milk prices. This was certainly a powerful incentive for voters to support the initiative, and in this sense the ballot issue held the promise of another strategic coup by the libertarians. Yet when the vote came, the measure failed. It seemed clear that most voters had heard the message about this being a chance to lower milk prices, and many responded by voting for the measure. But an even larger number seemed to have been swayed by another set of arguments, which in the end were more important to them than the prospect of lower milk prices. Local dairies had argued that decontrol would force them out of business by allowing giant out-of-state concerns to drive prices down until their local competition disappeared. Parallel arguments were made by a number of retailers. Small neighborhood grocery stores pointed out that milk control allowed them to charge the same prices for milk as the large chain stores did, whereas with most items, the smaller scale of the "mom and pop" operations forced them to charge higher prices. Milk had become a major segment of these small stores' trade, and they argued that if they lost this element of parity in milk, many of them would go out of business. Precisely the same argument was made by milk delivery businesses.

What was interesting about this particular vote was that it became a struggle between the abstract market and the marketplace. The libertarian appeal was to the highly individualistic instincts of "consumers"; the assumption was that their voting behavior would mirror their behavior within the market, that they would choose whatever brought them the lowest price. Many of them did, but a larger number of voters were motivated by a more complex range of factors. They voted to preserve family farms and local dairies, neighborhood stores and local milk delivery businesses. They did this knowing that they might have lowered milk prices by voting the other way. But obviously, to these people there were aspects of place, of loyalty to neighborhood and to neighbors, which outweighed their own purely individual motives.

The second ballot initiative which underscored the difference between a placeless market and a marketplace arose from the other end of the political spectrum, although its history was in many ways similar to the story of the libertarian-backed initiatives. In the early 1970s Montana, North Dakota, and Wyoming became the arena for a dramatic boom in coal production as energy companies began developing the low-sulfur Fort Union coal formation. The three states responded in various ways to these vast open-pit mines and the variety of challenges they posed. Reclamation and plant siting laws became major points of contention, as did the issue of coal severance taxes. All of the states passed such taxes, but Montana's, at 30 percent of the mine-mouth price of the coal, was considerably higher than the tax imposed by neighboring states.

As soon as Montana's severance tax was in place, the legislature placed on the ballot a constitutional referendum to put half of the tax revenues in a permanent trust fund. Soon after the trust fund was established, a handful of liberal legislators began a series of attempts to pass legislation requiring that a substantial portion of the trust fund be invested in the Montana economy. They argued that in the absence of such legislation, the money was invested solely according to the dictates of the national capital market, which meant that almost none of it was invested in Montana. Montana had a long history of being at the mercy of outside sources of capital, which had always meant that non-Montanans had the last word in how Montana's economy was developed (or failed to be developed). The coal boom was just one more chapter in that (essentially colonial) history.[6] But the establishment of the severance tax trust fund offered Montanans a pool of their own capital which, if wisely invested, could begin to develop Montana's economy on the state's own terms.

For three successive legislative sessions, bills were introduced to require that part of the trust fund be invested in Montana. Each time, the legislation was defeated. Opposition came from two quarters. The managers of the trust fund itself argued that they were required to get the highest possible monetary return on the money invested, and this, they argued, required them to follow the dictates of the national capital market. Meanwhile, the state's lending institutions, especially those controlled by out-of-state holding companies, argued that the state should not try to guide money into the Montana economy through political control of capital. If there were good investments to be made in Montana, the market would find them, they argued.

After three unsuccessful efforts to pass this legislation, its supporters went directly to the people with a ballot initiative. There, the same arguments which had been heard in the legislature were repeated, but the response was very different. The initiative passed by more than a two-to-one margin. As with the milk initiative, the issue here boiled down to a choice between a totally placeless, abstract market on the one hand (offering lower milk prices or higher returns on state investments) or, on the other hand, a place-centered market offering nurture and support for locally owned enterprises. In both cases, the voters had opted for the marketplace solution.

The in-state investment initiative and other coal tax–related programs offer a glimpse at what a re-inhabitory economics, a place-focused market, might look like in its early stages. The key to the in-state investment initiative was its emphasis on using Montana-generated capital for indigenous businesses. As Jane Jacobs argues, this is a key plank in any realistic program for building economies. Jacobs uses the example of Taiwan to show how localized capital formation, if it is used to promote import substitution, can build a strong economy:

> The events behind Taiwan's extraordinary and perhaps even unique achievements go back to 1956, when the government there introduced a program called Land to the Tiller. Its purpose, not in itself unusual, was to transfer agricultural soil from the ownership of feudal-like landlords to the peasants who worked the land. The government, in paying the expropriated landlords, attached a string to payments, however, a string that converted rural landlords into city capitalists. It stipulated investments of part of the payments in light industry. What kinds and where they would be were left up to the former landlords, as long as the investments were in Taiwan.[7]

Jacobs contrasts this approach to a less entrepreneurial, more bureaucratic alternative:

> Instead of paying off the expropriated landlords, the government could, of course, have used equivalent funds to set up light industries itself. But if it had done so, it seems inconceivable that these could have been as improvisational, flexible and diverse as those that actually were set up, or that they could conceivably have given rise to the schools of breakaway firms they have spawned by the thousands as employees, gaining experience, have discovered more niches in the economy, and customers, suppliers and investors for enterprises of their own.[8]

Jacobs concludes that keeping indigenous capital at home is a good way to begin building local economies, because, in effect, the capital knows the place: "Maybe what happened in Taiwan can't be replicated elsewhere. Maybe the improvisation of city capital that worked there wouldn't work out in another place. But this is the nature of successful economic improvisation of any sort: if it works, it isn't because it is abstractly or theoretically 'the right thing' but because it is actually practical for the time, the place, and the resources and opportunities at hand."[9]

Montana's approach to in-state investment was built, roughly, on the same philosophy. Both the citizens' initiative and the ensuing legislation required that for this portion of the trust fund, investment preference must be given to genuinely indigenous businesses. Administrative rules even specified that a capacity for import substitution would be one of the factors considered in deciding whether or not to invest in a particular enterprise. Once the in-state investment program was in place, it began to serve as a kind of anchor for a number of other programs which were also consistent with a place-oriented market. The Montana Department of Commerce, for example, launched a program to promote products which had been manufactured in Montana, with the objective of persuading Montanans, whenever possible, to buy Montana-made rather than imported goods. Such a program is obviously in keeping with the philosophy that import substitution is a key ingredient of economic growth.

Even before the in-state investment program had been enacted, the original coal tax legislation had made some forays into the promotion of a place-focused market. A small percentage of the coal tax revenues had been earmarked for investment in renewable energy research, development, and commercialization. Some of this capital eventually found its way into the place-specific complex of Missoula's energy market. As Missoula wrestled with the question of how it might use wood, a locally produced fuel, without destroying its airshed, coal tax money was invested in research and development of clean-burning wood pellet technology and marketing techniques. This was only one of dozens of examples of how Montana's decision to keep some coal-generated capital at home was leading to the development of place-specific markets in various Montana communities.

These economic development initiatives may all be seen as efforts to build an economy matched to its place. Such an economy would keep locally or regionally generated capital at home, investing it in indigenous businesses, encouraging both import substitution and economic activity which respects the integrity of the local environment. In these terms, programs like Montana's in-state investment program or similar projects in other states may be understood as halting moves in the direction of an inhabitory economics or a place-focused market. But certainly the emphasis here must be placed upon the word *halting*. The later history of Montana's coal tax illustrates the uncertainties attending these forays into the marketplace.

For a decade after its enactment, Montana's coal tax was the most popular element of the state's agenda. The popularity of the tax reached its peak when national forces began attacking the severance tax in the courts and in Congress. Coal companies and utilities challenged the tax in federal court, arguing that it interfered impermissibly with interstate commerce. In a major affirmation of states' rights in the economic arena, the U.S. Supreme Court ruled in 1982 that unless Congress specifically limited state severance taxes, the states were not constitutionally prevented from imposing them.[10] The battle then shifted to Congress, where the same industries sought to impose limits on the capacity of states to tax the extraction of natural resources.

Subsequent events defused this congressional battle before it reached any resolution, but the issue of state taxation power over natural resource extraction is likely to arise again. It is an issue which brings into focus many of the principal features of re-inhabitory, or place-centered, economics. If places (especially places in the West) are to gain any real control over their own economies—if they are to gain any capacity to encourage indigenous businesses—then they must have the ability to keep some locally generated capital within the region. The essentially colonial history of this region has been a result of its dependence upon markets (both commodity and capital markets) which do not center in this place but which treat the place as an object for their use, if not exploitation. Economic self-determination would require that the region, or localities within the region, develop place-centered markets for both capital and commodities. But in the West, any substantial capital generation must be based upon natural resource extraction, simply because there are so few other major indigenous sources of capital. If states cannot impose reasonable levels of severance taxes, then, their capacity to keep some locally generated capital at home would be seriously damaged.

What would stop states from using this means of building their own economies? What threatened to stop Montana, both in the courts and in Congress, was the Interstate Commerce Clause of the U.S. Constitution. It is this clause, above all, that has made real the idea that the nation is the preeminent locus of the economy. The Interstate Commerce Clause presumes that the national economy is supreme, just as federal law is supreme, and that state or local economies must subordinate their own activities to the imperatives of the national economy. The national argument against state severance taxes is that there is a national market in something like coal, and that states, by imposing severance taxes, have the capacity to interfere with that market. This is substantially the same argument as the one used by the opponents of Montana's in-state investment program; they, too, were arguing that Montana policy should not interfere with national markets (in that case, capital markets).

There is nothing new about any of this. The 1787 Constitutional Convention itself was called largely to respond to the growing clamor to create a national economy and to protect it against the actions of states, which were trying to build their own economies. If there is anything new in the current situation, it is the growing recognition that the idea of a national economy may be seriously flawed—that the nation may be either too small or too big (or maybe both) to be an effective locus for "the economy." As states and localities become more interested in developing their own economies, the inherent conflict between those efforts and the notion of the supremacy of the national economy is likely to grow more and more acute. States rights battles (like those which the

West has fought over severance taxes) are an almost inevitable outcome of any serious effort to establish effective local or regional economies.

But even without any heavy-handed imposition of national supremacy, the path toward place-centered economies is steep and rocky. The history of Montana's coal severance tax may again be used to illustrate the point. In the end, the national economy did not have to protect itself against Montana by invoking congressional power over interstate commerce. Instead, the national (or international) market, by its own weight, lowered the Montana tax and eliminated the need for congressional action. By 1985, a decade after the adoption of the severance tax, the nation had built itself into a position of substantial energy surplus, especially with regard to electricity. Because so much of the region's coal production was targeted toward the generation of electricity, slowing the growth rate of electric production had to (and did) dampen the coal market. At the same time, the oil exporting nations had let oil prices fall, further depressing the market for coal.

These two forces created a situation in which Montana, for the first time in many years, saw no new coal mines being opened. What had been the fastest-growing sector of the state's (and the region's) economy suddenly assumed a steady-state posture. In an effort to induce new growth, state politicians began attempting what the state had so ardently resisted when outsiders proposed it: lowering the Montana severance tax. By 1987, the legislature had enacted a program which would eventually cut the coal tax in half.

If the adoption of the coal tax and its investment in the Montana economy had been a move in the direction of re-inhabitory economics, then this response to market pressures should probably be called "de-inhabitory." The original imposition of the severance tax had been, on several levels, an effort to shape the economy to fit the place. There had been a recognition, for example, that an activity like coal mining places many burdens on the land and on local communities, which the activity itself should help to pay for. The policy makers who adopted the severance tax had also recognized that coal production marked one more in a long series of stories about extraction of this region's natural resources—a series which had always, in the past, left later generations of the region's inhabitants with a smaller resource base from which to draw a living. This time, the state had decided, the extraction of the resource would leave behind a legacy of wealth, in the form of a trust fund, to help meet the needs of later generations.

Both in responding to the needs of future generations and in seeking to meet the more immediate effects of mining, the policy makers had argued, in effect, that the imperatives of place should play a role in shaping the market. An economist might have said that Montanans were deciding to internalize some of the externalities of coal production—to make the market price of coal more nearly reflective of the real costs of producing the coal. This is simply another way to bring place into the market—by insisting that the market respond to the place in a realistic way. But in the end, Montana bowed to the abstract, placeless market by saying that the first priority was to sell coal and to price it so it would sell in the market, leaving the place to care for itself as best it could.

This entire story of resource extraction, and of the faltering efforts to gain local or regional control over it, should be understood as part of the history of the American frontier. The economic history of America has been as closely tied as was our constitutional history to the development of the frontier. We have already seen that the frontier was, in a sense, built into the Constitution; the frontier was part of the largely unspoken plan for "keeping citizens apart" upon which the Constitution rested. This in turn created a situation in which the relationship of Americans to place was always ambivalent, at best—an ambivalence which Hegel identified quite precisely. If domestic tranquility in America depended upon the capacity of people to escape each other, then place must be, for most Americans most of the time, merely something to pass through. What Hegel argued was that America would only become "civil-ized" when it no longer had any place to escape to—when Americans "shall have begun to be pressed back on each other," forced to come to terms with each other. Which is to say that public life would begin when inhabitation became a serious, common enterprise.

A large part of the enterprise of inhabitation is economic—it is a matter of recognizing that a particular place is "the household" which must be managed—the finite, bounded setting within which the age-old interplay of scarcity and possibility, which we call the economy, may unfold itself. But just as America, by declaring itself a nation with a seemingly infinite frontier, had postponed the project of coming to terms with itself civically, so had it, by declaring that the economy would be national, postponed the project of economic inhabitation. Economically, as well as politically, "the nation" was not a place, but a denial of place. Wendell Berry captures the essence of the situation in what he calls "the unsettling of America:"

> One of the peculiarities of the white race's presence in America is how little intention has been applied to it. As a people, wherever we have been, we have never really intended to be. The continent is said to have been discovered by an Italian who was on his way to India. The earliest explorers were looking for gold, which was, after an early streak of luck in Mexico, always somewhere further on. Conquests and foundings were incidental to this search—which did not, and could not, end until the continent was finally laid open in an orgy of goldseeking in the middle of the last century. Once the unknown of geography was mapped, the industrial marketplace became the new frontier, and we continued, with largely the same motives and with increasing haste and anxiety, to displace ourselves—no longer with unity of direction, like a migrant flock, but more like the refugees from a broken ant hill.[11]

The mineral-rich region of the Northern Rockies provided a major arena for the "orgy of goldseeking in the middle of the last century." As such, this region has for over a century been particularly subject to America's devotion to its own placelessness. The wealth that was extracted from this part of the earth was always extracted by and for the placeless market. This region, therefore, never developed its own marketplace, its own economy. To that extent, it has not yet been inhabited. Instead, it has played a major part in the unsettling of America.

Yet as Wendell Berry points out, the frontier commitment to placelessness has never been the whole story, and certainly not the whole story in this region: "To be just, . . . it is necessary to remember that there has been another tendency: the tendency to stay put, to say, 'No farther. This is the place.' So far, this has been the weaker tendency, less glamorous, certainly less successful. It is also the older of these tendencies, having been the dominant one among the Indians." [12]

The ups and downs of the Montana coal tax reflect the continuing ambivalence of this region about its own place. On the one hand, there has been a willingness to intervene with the abstract market, either in coal or in capital, to make it conform to the imperatives of the place. On the other hand, there has been submission to the dictates of that abstract market. Ideals like building strong, stable local economies by encouraging import substitution, or nurturing indigenous businesses, cannot go far in this part of the country unless colonial patterns are interrupted. Specifically, the building of strong, indigenous communities requires that states and localities have the capacity and the will to keep some locally generated capital from leaving the region and to invest that capital creatively and effectively in the regional economy. A number of implications arise from this premise.

First, the presumption of the supremacy of the national market must be selectively challenged. In part, as we have seen, this is a matter of states' rights. Specifically, state taxation power must not be so restricted by judicial or congressional applications of the Interstate Commerce Clause that states lose their capacity to build their own economies. But states, too, must be prepared to share economic sovereignty in an unaccustomed way. If in fact, as Jane Jacobs argues, cities and their regions are inherently the most potent economic entities, then states must be willing to share economic development tools (including taxation powers and control over capital) with cities. Finally, if city regions are to be economically empowered, then it will often happen that those regions will cross state lines. If these regional, interstate economies are to realize their full potential, a whole new flexible and creative range of instrumentalities for interlocal and interstate cooperation will have to be developed.

The development of place-focused economies will require other forms of cooperation as well. To understand this, consider once again Missoula's struggle with wood-smoke pollution. If the Missoula Valley is to enjoy the benefits of using a local fuel source (wood) without fouling its airshed, a number of groups and individuals will have to develop some new and stable patterns of cooperation. Such cooperative patterns are not uniquely applicable to the Missoula Valley; they reflect, in fact, some fundamental features of any place-centered economy. But precisely because it is place-centered, this economic cooperation must be described in terms of particular places and their particular circumstances.

From the time that wood smoke was first identified as a major source of the valley's air pollution, there has been a steady shift from the use of cord wood to wood pellets as a fuel source. Pellets, which are produced by compressing finely pulverized wood chips, burn much more cleanly and efficiently than cord wood, but they do require specialized equipment, which is somewhat more expensive than conventional wood stoves. Faced on the one hand with regulations which prohibit the burning of wood during temperature inversions in anything but very clean stoves, and on the other with the higher cost of the clean-burning stoves, most families or individuals will be inclined to switch (often very grudgingly) to a nonrenewable fuel source. This behavior is exactly what a placeless market will produce in response to these particular regulations. More money and jobs leave the local economy, and more people come to resent how "the government" interferes in their lives. In these and other ways, the uneasy conjunction of individualism and regulation, within the framework of an abstract market, leaves the community poorer and weaker, both economically and politically. But a real market*place*, focused upon the place-centered dynamic of import substitution, may produce a different set of behaviors and a wealthier and stronger community.

But how would it do this? Clean-burning stoves would still be expensive; the individual consumer, faced with the choice of making this substantial capital outlay or switching to an imported fuel, would still be concerned first of all with the family budget. But it is precisely here that cooperation becomes central to inhabitation. Neither pure individualism nor bureaucratic regulation can create an economy "to match its scenery." Wallace Stegner was exactly correct: only cooperation can do this. Thus, for example, if the people of Missoula could agree among themselves, they might do what Boise, Idaho has done: they might create a revolving loan fund which would enable people to buy clean-burning stoves on reasonable terms. No individual consumer is in a position to affect the situation in this way; only a cooperative act of the entire community (or some substantial part of it) can solve this problem.

But even if they had affordable financing to enable them to buy pellet-burning equipment, many families would not be willing to invest in pellet stoves unless they were certain that pellets were going to continue to be available. Because natural gas or electricity is publicly regulated, a person can be fairly certain that an investment in a gas or electric heating system will not be vulnerable in this way. But investment in a pellet stove does not carry this bureaucratic protection. What is the solution to this problem? One promising possibility would be a consumer-owned cooperative. Such cooperatives have traditionally arisen in response to precisely this set of circumstances, in which consumers have to make a fairly substantial capital outlay and are best able to guard that investment by cooperatively owning the production facilities. An example of this is the rural electric cooperative which Albert and Lilly and the rest of their neighbors formed to bring electricity to their remote corner of Montana. None of those farmers, acting alone, could bring electricity to their farms any more than they could build their barns by acting alone. Inhabiting that place at that time was something that individuals simply as individuals could not accomplish. Burning wood in Missoula is also an inhabitory response to a place and a time, but it also increasingly presents itself as something that no one can do simply as an individual.

It is not only consumers who might have to learn to cooperate in order to meet this particular challenge. This region is dotted with small sawmills, which have suffered a gradual erosion over the years as the severe business cycles of the wood products industry have progressively driven out the smaller mills. Operating closer and closer to the margin, these locally owned mills must grasp any opportunity to make their operations more efficient. One of their problems is sawdust: it cannot be burned or disposed of in any other way, so it piles up and eventually fills all of the spare land around the plant. It becomes an expense, threatening to cut still further the dangerously slender profit margin of these small mills. One of the only uses that has been found for this waste is the manufacture of wood pellets. When a newspaper story revealed that a local economic development council was working on a study on wood pellets, the group was contacted by a number of owners of small mills, all with the same question: Could they install a pellet plant at their mill? All of them saw this as an opportunity to solve a waste problem and increase their perilously slim profit margin. But the answer in every case had to be that the amount of waste that any one mill produced would not support an economically sized pellet plant. Again, the possibility of a cooperative approach—this time a suppliers' co-op—began to emerge.

Here again, the distinction between a placeless market and a marketplace is evident. The abstract market solution to the waste wood problem might be for a separately owned pellet plant simply to enter into individual contracts with each of the small sawmills to take their waste wood. But this may not be the best solution for the place itself. One reason that the sawmill owners were interested in

making pellets was that it would enable them to get rid of some
waste and make a modest profit from the manufacture of pellets in
the bargain. The profit margin of these small mills is important not
only to the sawmill owners themselves, but also to the larger community, which is generally thought to be better off with several
smaller mills in operation rather than having the entire industry
centralized in one large plant. But here is a situation in which, if all
the small operators simply attempt, on their own, to maximize their
profits, none of them are likely to succeed. Competing against each
other to sell their sawdust may leave them all with a very low income
from that source. On the other hand, if they could form a suppliers'
cooperative, they might themselves share in the profits of the pellet
plant. These small producers, then, are in the same position as the
individual consumers: only by some form of cooperative merging of
their individual interests can any of those interests be maximized.

We see, then, in some fairly concrete ways how it may be true
that the creation of a real marketplace, an economy of inhabitation,
may require the development of some new practices of cooperation.
But how will those practices emerge, and what will nurture them?
Even if they are, as Stegner implies, native to this soil, they do not
seem to flourish automatically; they require human nurturing, fore-
thought, and intention. What they require, in fact, is a politics which
is as place-focused, as inhabitory, and finally as cooperative as the
economy of place. Only such a political culture would be effective
in encouraging Missoula's wood-burning families or western Montana's small sawmills to engage in the kind of cooperation which
would enable Missoula and its surrounding region to realize the
benefits of import substitution. But the need for such a politics
extends further. We spoke earlier of the necessity for states, regions,
and localities to resist some of the pressures of the placeless market
as they attempt to strengthen and stabilize their own economies.
Montana's retreat on the issue of coal severance taxes demonstrates
how persuasive those de-inhabitory market pressures can be. Here
again, the development of strong indigenous economies is incon-

ceivable apart from some political changes which would give regions and localities the political will to assert their own long-term interests. The economics of inhabitation cannot succeed without the development of some new political practices.

Notes

1. Jane Jacobs, *Cities and the Wealth of Nations*, p. 35.
2. Ibid.
3. Ibid., p. 39.
4. Ibid., p. 42
5. Ibid., p. 38
6. See K. Ross Toole, *Montana: An Uncommon Land; Twentieth Century Montana: A State of Extremes*; and *Rape of the Great Plains.*
7. Jane Jacobs, *Cities and the Wealth of Nations*, pp. 99–100.
8. Ibid., p. 101
9. Ibid., pp. 101–102.
10. *Commonwealth Edison Company* v. *Montana*, 453 U.S. 609 (1982).
11. Wendell Berry, *The Unsettling of America*, p. 3.
12. Ibid., p. 4.

CHAPTER EIGHT

The Art of the Possible
in the Home of Hope
(The Politics of Re-Inhabitation)

A familiar maxim defines politics as "the art of the possible." This
definition is often invoked to end debates by reminding someone
that the proper realm of politics is not the ideal, but the real: the
restricted realm of what is, in fact, possible. But referring to politics
as the art of the possible might also be a way of invoking the
possibilities inhering in the world—a way of drawing attention to
what is not, but could be. Robert Kennedy caught the essence of
this way of viewing politics with his often-used quote from George
Bernard Shaw: "You see things; and you say, "Why?" But I dream
things that never were, and I say, "Why not?" [1] Politics as "the art
of the possible," in other words, may mean that "the glass is half
empty," but it may also mean that "the glass is half full." I do not
want to argue that the second sense of the definition should be
entirely substituted for the first, but simply that politics should be
understood as "the art of the possible" in both of these senses. It is
the tension between these two meanings which makes politics interesting—which makes it, indeed, a human enterprise.

Something resembling the more expansive sense of politics as the
art of the possible is frequently remarked upon by observers of the
West. When Wallace Stegner calls the West "the native home of

hope," he identifies an enduring sense of possibility which seems to dwell in this place. Political pollster Peter Hart, summarizing a comparative regional survey of political attitudes, has noted that "polls in Western states show the region's residents to be more optimistic and possess more of a 'can do' attitude than people in any other region." Western politicians, Hart says, "campaign in the shadow of spectacular snow-capped vistas, and revel in what Sen. Orrin G. Hatch calls 'a feeling of freedom in the West, the wide-open spaces, the opportunity and joy of life that you just don't find elsewhere.'"[2] Somehow, open vistas seem to encourage a more expansive or hopeful attitude. It will be remembered that Wallace Stegner makes his remark about the "native home of hope" in the context of predicting the continued existence of some open land in the West and of trying to imagine for the West "a society to match its scenery." For Stegner, open country and open possibilities seem to go hand in hand. These observations are perhaps only modern ways of paraphrasing a terse declaration of Frederick Jackson Turner's: "So long as free land exists, the opportunity for a competency exists. . . ."[3] This "competency" of Turner's frontier echoes still in Hart's "can-do attitude" native to "wide-open spaces."

This "competency," this sense of opportunity and hope, is where politics as the art of the possible should find its sustenance. Yet by and large, the politics of the West is far less a matter of "opportunity and the joy of life" than, as William Janklow says, a matter of "anybody wrecking anything." Despite the wide vistas of the physical landscape, the horizons of western politics, like the horizons of politics elsewhere, have been drastically narrowed by the deadlocking practices of the procedural republic. As Lawrence Goodwyn writes of the politics of post-frontier America, "The narrowed boundaries of modern politics . . . outline a clear retreat from the democratic vistas of either the eighteenth-century Jeffersonians or the nineteenth-century Populists."[4]

Yet there are signs, more numerous all the time, of a resurgence of possibilities, of a capacity to get things done, which may yet reclaim the diminishing sense of a politics of possibility. Perhaps the time has come to lift our gaze to the far horizons, to open up the boundaries of politics, to begin the hard but endlessly rewarding job of creating, here, in the native home of hope, a politics to match our vistas. We need to begin to imagine what a politics of possibility might look like.

There are two levels upon which this transforming work must occur. On the individual level, it requires a revitalized sense of what might be meant by "citizenship." On the level of the body politic, it implies a renewed understanding of the *polis.* Each of these levels of political renewal deserves some careful attention. We will begin with the concept of citizenship, approaching it, again, by way of a story.

Recently, a group called the Down Home Project went to the Missoula city council with a request for a community development block grant to help construct a community solar greenhouse. The greenhouse would provide both work and food for a variety of constituencies, including developmentally disabled, elderly, and un-employed people. Modeled after a successful project in Cheyenne, Wyoming, the greenhouse had built strong support from various groups within the community and was well on its way to gaining the support of the city council. Then, at the last minute, the project came to a standstill.

The plans had called for a laundromat to be attached to the greenhouse to provide both backup heat and operating funds for the project. There was no laundromat on Missoula's North Side, so the idea seemed feasible. But as the final hearing date approached, the laundromat owners from across Missoula became alarmed, con-tacted each other, and began calling city hall. I heard about all this when Kerry Wall-MacLane, the director of the Down Home Proj-ect, called me and asked if I would mediate a meeting between Down Home and the laundromat owners.

The tension around the table at the Elks Club that evening was thick enough to float a horseshoe. These people did not understand, like, or trust each other. I gave a little homily about treating each other like neighbors rather than enemies, and then rang the bell for round one. After Wall-MacLane explained what the project was all about, I asked the laundromat owners to say why they were upset. Their reason was not surprising: they didn't want public funds to be used to build a competing laundromat.

Once that case had been clearly made, one of the more outspoken owners turned to me and said, "Now, you've been in the legislature; you're part of the government; what do you think about this?" His tone made it clear that he expected, now that the opposing ideologies had been laid on the table, that it was time for someone "in government" to choose between them. I insisted, however, that the question was not what I thought, but what the Down Home people thought. The owners were not very satisfied with that response, but they did turn their attention back to Wall-MacLane.

He said, with obvious sincerity, that he understood their concern about unfair competition and wanted to be responsive to it, but that he also wanted them to understand his dilemma. As they listened to Wall-MacLane, they started to acknowledge the value of the greenhouse project as well as the months of effort and the genuine expectations that were resting on this grant. I urged both sides to try to think of compromise approaches, and they worked in that direction in good faith, but they could not find a way to resolve the impasse. Finally, Wall-MacLane simply acknowledged that the arguments of the owners were sound and said that, while he thought he could hold enough votes on the city council, he could not in good conscience go forward with the proposal.

Now clearly taken aback, the laundromat owners began trying to think of alternate ways for Down Home to generate income or to think of ways that they could support the project. Several of them said that the city itself should support such projects, even if it meant somewhat higher taxes (a position that none of these free-enterprisers would likely have taken at the beginning of the evening). As the meeting broke up, one of the owners came to me and said, "I never felt worse about winning in my life."

If this issue had gone to public hearing, the results would have been different, in a number of ways. First, the Down Home director was probably right: he no doubt had enough committed votes to weather the storm. The laundromat owners would then have become more disenchanted with city government, and with government in general, than they already were. Whichever side won, they would not likely have come out of the hearing feeling or acting upon any sense of responsibility to the losing side. Whether the laundromat owners won or lost, they would not have found themselves thinking that perhaps city government should be funding projects like this from general revenues.

It is the issue of responsibility that sets this kind of collaborative approach off from the normal public hearing. Once the parties themselves get the idea that they are responsible for coming up with the answer, rather than simply turning it over to a third party, they are very likely to begin to think and behave differently. In this instance, the major shouldering of responsibility was done by the Down Home Project. Rather than leave it to the city council to decide whether the arguments about unfair competition were sound or not, these people rather courageously took that responsibility themselves. There seems to be something inherently mutual about the taking of responsibility; it is difficult not to respond to it. The laundromat owners clearly were responding—in their efforts to think of alternatives, in their willingness to consider a new perspective on government programs, and even in their feeling some real sorrow about the result.

This kind of mediated, participatory approach to problems is happening more and more frequently in an ever wider array of situations. Wherever it does happen, people find themselves being responsible for the ultimate decision, for each other, and even for their own ideologies in ways that they may never have experienced before. This taking of responsibility is the precise opposite of the move toward the "unencumbered self." It is, quite simply, the development of citizenship. As people learn to relate in this way to each other, they discover in their patterns of relationship a new competence, an unexpected capacity to get things done. It is not getting things done by using bureaucracies or other instrumentalities of "the government," but getting things done through the power of citizenship.

In 1984, the large pulp mill outside Missoula found that its settling ponds were reaching their capacity, so the mill's managers asked the state for permission to discharge some mill waste into the Clark Fork River. A new environmental group was formed in response to this situation, and it soon asked the Montana Water Quality Bureau to perform a more extensive environmental impact statement. This, of course, implied a series of public hearings. The procedural republic was gearing up, with all its potential for two-by-four debates, deadlock, and alienation. But then the pulp mill managers and the environmental group began talking to each other. The plant manager described how warily he had gone into those talks. "We'd had experience with environmental groups before," he said. "We'd learned not to trust them, because it seemed that every time they were given the slightest concession, they simply used it as a new foothold to ask for more concessions. We thought the same thing was going to happen this time." But in fact, it was different this time. Eventually, the two sides were able to agree on a solution which they jointly presented to the Water Quality Bureau. The plant manager was very clear about the crucial element which made this result possible. It was the gradual building of a sense of trust between the parties. Moving slowly, a small step at a time, the parties had gradually demonstrated to one another their good faith and reliability, to the point that they were able to trust each other to make a joint presentation to the decision maker. By that time, they had themselves in effect become the decision makers, but only because they had been willing to move together into the unoccupied territory of collaboration.

It is in events like this that public life is being and will be regenerated in this country. A couple of features of this event should be underscored. First is the indispensable element of trust. This is one of those civic virtues which people like Jefferson had argued were essential to public life, but which the procedural republic does not depend upon (and does not nurture). Second is the fact that such civic virtues can only become a constitutive feature of public life in one way: through practice. Trust, for example, is not very likely to be learned from a book, or even from a very good sermon. Trust, in other words, cannot be learned from words alone; it must largely be learned from work, as Paulo Freire argues: "Trust is contingent on the evidence which one party provides the others of his true, concrete intentions; it cannot exist if that party's words do not coincide with his actions." [5]

This kind of collaboration is part of what Robert Reich calls "the next American frontier." [6] The manager of this same pulp mill helped me to understand why that may be an appropriate image. This executive had just returned from a training session at the Harvard Negotiation Project. He had gone to prepare for a round of labor contract negotiations, but he had returned believing that the principles of the workshop were also applicable to a much broader range of situations, including environmental conflicts. He drew me a picture, to show me what he was so enthusiastic about:

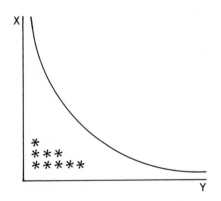

The plant manager explained to me that X and Y are participants in an adversarial situation of some kind. The asterisks grouped down in the corner of the graph represent the range of solutions which are attainable by either party through adversarial means. The curved line is the limit of solutions achievable by collaborative methods of problem-solving. The space between the actual solutions and the potential ones is the unoccupied territory. For this corporate executive, as for Robert Reich, this territory represents "the next American frontier."

But from the outset, this is a very strange kind of frontier. Its one inescapable characteristic is that it can only be occupied by adversaries venturing into the territory together. Either party, alone, cannot occupy the territory. This is country where Wallace Stegner's formula is absolutely fundamental; this is territory where "cooperation, not rugged individualism, is the quality which most characterizes and preserves it."[7]

Reich is not alone in referring to this new approach to public life in terms of a new frontier. George Will, for example, argues that we can open up a new frontier by rejecting the faulty premises of the Madisonian procedural republic:

> A theme of modern American historiography is that something epochal occurred about 1890 when the frontier was "closed." Certainly something changed—some source of energy, some agreeable itch or tingle in the nation's soul—when the age of physical exploration ended. But . . . a nation is not a physical thing. A nation offers limitless scope for moral explorations. . . . In politics "the place" is a mental habitat, an intellectual and moral landscape. To know clearly, perhaps even for the first time, the defective philosophic premises of our nation should not mean loving the nation less. . . . Because a nation is, to some extent, a state of mind, knowing a nation in a new way makes the nation into a new place.[8]

It might well be said that the emerging kind of citizenship, in which adversaries learn to solve problems through face-to-face collaboration, is a rejection of the syndrome of the "procedural republic and the unencumbered self" and therefore a rejection of the "defective philosophic premises of our nation." And if collaboration does allow such adversaries to move, together, into new arenas of possibility, then in an important way they occupy "a new place."

Yet it is important to keep in mind that the concept of "place" enters into this situation in a literal as well as a metaphorical way. The pulp mill and the local environmental group were brought to the point of collaboration because both of them had a stake in what happened to a particular place. They had different stakes, and had they been left to themselves, they would have done different things with the place, but in the end it was one and the same place. Neither party wanted to leave the place, and both recognized that what Lester Thurow says of territoriality in such a case is true: neither side could gain a decisive or lasting victory over the other (although they were both free to use the procedural republic in an attempt to win). Once they recognized that the procedural republic was not likely to serve them well, they were thrown back on collaboration (on citizenship). But what holds people together long enough to discover their power as citizens is their common inhabiting of a single place. No matter how diverse and complex the patterns of livelihood may be that arise within the river system, no matter how many the perspectives from which people view the basin, no matter how diversely they value it, it is, finally, one and the same river for everyone. There are not many rivers, one for each of us, but only this one river, and if we all want to stay here, in some kind of relation to the river, then we have to learn, somehow, to live together.

Before they become citizens, then, these people are neighbors; this is a neighborly citizenship. But by that I do not mean simply that it is folksy or friendly. The word *neighbor*, in its Old English rendition, meant something like "near dweller." Neighbors are essentially people who find themselves attached to the same (or nearly adjoining) places. Because each of them is attached to the place, they are brought into relationship with each other. As we saw in the barn building story, such people may actually prefer that they had different neighbors, but because neither of them is about to leave, and because their dwelling in this place makes them interdependent, they develop patterns for dwelling near each other, for living with each other.

This concept of "living with" is deeply rooted in various inhabitory practices. Consider, for example, the process by which the industrialists and the environmentalists on the Clark Fork worked out a solution to the waste discharge problem. Theirs was a process of consensus building, which has by now developed some fairly standard operating procedures. One of the guidelines that is often invoked in consensus decision making is that participants should be looking for solutions which they can all live with. Such an approach can be viewed simply as a matter of compromise and accomodation, and certainly it contains such elements. But the actual practice of finding solutions that people can live with usually reaches beyond compromise to something more like neighborliness—to finding within shared space the possibilities for a shared inhabitation. Such neighborliness is inconceivable without the building of trust, of some sense of justice, of reliability or honesty. This practice of being neighbors draws together, therefore, the concepts of place, of inhabitation, and of the kinds of practices from which civic virtues evolve.

Most people, most of the time, do not think about these features of the art of being good neighbors. What they do know is that neighborliness is a highly prized quality of life. Where it is present, it is always near the top of people's lists of why they like a place, and where it is absent, it is deeply lamented. This deep-seated attachment to the virtue of neighborliness is an important but largely ignored civic asset. It is in being good neighbors that people very often engage in those simple, homely practices which are the last, best hope for a revival of genuine public life. In valuing neighborliness, people value that upon which citizenship most essentially depends. It is our good fortune that this value persists.

So it is that places may play a role in the revival of citizenship. Places have a way of claiming people. When they claim very diverse kinds of people, then those people must eventually learn to live with each other; they must learn to inhabit their place together, which they can only do through the development of certain practices of inhabitation which both rely upon and nurture the old-fashioned civic virtues of trust, honesty, justice, toleration, cooperation, hope, and remembrance. It is through the nurturing of such virtues (and in no other way) that we might begin to reclaim that competency upon which democratic citizenship depends.

If this enterprise of inhabitation is at the root of any vital sense of democratic citizenship, then it is not surprising that it is also basic to the concept of politics itself. In *Strong Democracy*, Benjamin Barber evokes this inhabitory foundation of politics and things political: "To render a political judgment is not to exclaim 'I prefer' or 'I want' or 'I choose such and such' but rather to say, 'I will a world in which such and such is possible.' To decide is thus to will into being a world that the community must experience in common: it is to create a common future, if only for selfish ends." This willing of a common world (of the "public thing") is a radically different approach to public life from the procedural republic's brokering of individual interests: "Interests can all coexist in the world of reflective reason; one is as good as the next. But wills cannot all be equally legitimate in the same sense, because by willing one affects the world, and the world is finally one—our world. . . . With interest, we may ask: 'Do you prefer A or B or C?' With wills, we must ask: 'What sort of world do you will our common world to be?' " [9]

This "common world" which political will creates is the *res publica*, the "public thing." When this willing of a common world is understood in terms of inhabitation, it becomes clear that the common world which we will and which we inhabit must always be some mixture of the natural and the altered or fabricated. The political question becomes *what* mixture we choose. But the matter is obviously complicated, for if the common world is a mixture of the natural and the altered, then our power to shape that world extends only to part of it—namely, to the humanly altered or fabricated part. What we can choose about the natural part is only to leave it natural, or to move it to the other side of the ledger. These choices, as we well know, are a major part of our political enterprise, particularly in the West. But the willing of our common world then becomes a kind of joint venture in which humans will part of the world and agree among themselves to allow nature to shape the remainder.

This sharing of responsibility between the human and the natural extends also to the question of the scope or scale of the political entity. Over what domain is political will to be exercised? In our time, we have come to assume that answering this question is strictly a human responsibility. So humans draw lines on the land, marking off nations, states, and counties. But as the challenge of inhabitation makes itself felt in the political sphere, it becomes clear that this drawing of lines should not, perhaps, be left entirely to human choice. Too often, the lines cut across natural units of inhabitation, leaving inhabitants cut off from each other in terms of their capacity to act together politically—to will a common world.

This assumes that there are such things as "natural units of inhabitation" which lend themselves to the political act of willing a common world. We are familiar with such units of inhabitation for non-human life; they are what we call "ecosystems." The root of *ecosystem* is the same Greek word, *oikos*, ("household") which stands at the root of the word *economy*. In fact, these two households may have more in common than we generally realize—a commonality which we may have to recognize in order actually to practice a politics of willing a common world. The first step is to recognize that there is, at least potentially, a kind of organic household consisting of both natural and humanly appropriated elements, within which inhabitation is a genuine possibility.

This is precisely Jane Jacobs' argument in *Cities and the Wealth of Nations*. When Jacobs argues that city regions are the natural economic entities, she is speaking of a natural, symbiotic relationship between cities, the almost entirely fabricated element, and their largely natural hinterlands. If left to themselves, Jacobs argues, cities and their hinterlands will establish a natural, healthy balance. But if this is so, then it may well be that cities are not only the primary economic units but also the basic political entities. In other words, it may be that the boundaries which humans draw across landscapes create artificial and inefficient units both in economic and in political terms. If cities, in relation to their hinterlands, have the capacity to define working economies, then it makes sense that the same city regions which constitute economies should also be "city-states"— the manageable households within which the task of willing a common world takes place.

This suggestion is almost totally out of tune with modern political theory and practice, but it would not have sounded odd at all to many an earlier age. We have come to treat cities as purely derivative, the neglected stepchildren of state and nation. Politically we have no experience whatever of "city regions" or "city-states." Yet from its very inception, politics has been rooted precisely where Jacobs argues that economics is rooted: in the city region, or the city-state—the *polis*—which is the root of all politics.

In his elegant little book *The Needs of Strangers*, Michael Ignatieff pays tribute to this essence of politics:

> Whenever I try to imagine a future other than the one towards which we seem to be hurtling, I find myself dreaming a dream of the past. It is the vision of the classical *polis*—the city-state of ancient Greece and renaissance Italy—which beckons me backwards, as it were, into the future. No matter that Greek democracy was built upon the institution of slavery; no matter that the Italian city-states were feuding and unequal oligarchies. Utopias never have to make their excuses to history; like all dreams they have a timeless immunity to disappointment in real life. The *polis* would continue to beckon us forward out of the past even if no actual *polis* had ever existed.[10]

At least part of the reason the *polis* has this enduring paradigmatic power is because of the way it focuses our attention on the shared enterprise of inhabitation. The *polis* is, first of all, the place which a certain group of people recognize that they inhabit in common. Any individual or any group within that place may wish that others did not live there, but they recognize that removing them would, in one way or another, exact too high a price. Given that fact, politics emerges as the set of practices which enables these people to dwell together in this place.[11] Not the set of procedures, not the set of laws or rules or regulations, but the set of practices which enables a common inhabiting of a common place.

It is no accident at all that the very concept of practice (what the Greeks named *praxis*) arose in the context of the *polis*. The common willing of a common world is an eminently practical undertaking, not in the least abstract. As Barber says, the result of the exercise is always *this* world, this actual, physical setting, these precise relationships among and between these people and this place. Rules and laws certainly have their role in the *polis*, but in the end they are, by their very nature, abstractions from the particular, the concrete. Procedures and rules arrive at the common by abstracting from the particular; practices arrive at the common *through* the particular, through a shared way of arranging and relating to the actual, physical world—"our world."

In the valley of the Clark Fork, the plant managers and the environmentalists had plenty of procedures available to them, which they might have used to determine the conditions of their living together in the valley. But those procedures are increasingly unsatisfactory for a number of reasons, not least because their use over a series of situations produces a result which is less satisfactory than any of the participants would have chosen. The plant manager's graph tells the story which impelled these people in the direction of citizenship and of politics: the range of procedural solutions is less satisfying to all parties than a collaborative solution is likely to be. Thus, in a number of settings, people who find themselves held together (perhaps against their will) in a shared place discover as well that their best possibility for realizing the potential of the place is to learn to work together. In this way places breed cooperation, and out of this ancient relationship of place to human willing, that specific activity which is rightly called "politics" is born.

But what odd implications this all carries for America, and for this region which was the last of America's old frontier. This kind of politics implies at one and the same time a rejection of both of the fundamental federalist premises which underlay the U.S. Constitution. A politics of citizens working out the problems and the possibilities of their place directly among themselves implies a revival of the old republican notion of citizenship based upon civic virtue; it rejects the federalist use of procedures to "supply the defect of better motives." But a politics which rests upon a mutual recognition by diverse interests that they are bound to each other by their common attachment to a place also rejects the notion of a politics of "keeping citizens apart." Escaping from each other into frontiers of any kind is explicitly rejected. But it is not only the Madisonian version of the "expanding sphere" which this politics of inhabitation denies. It also differs very substantially from Jefferson's view of republican politics as being antithetical to the establishment of cities. A politics of inhabitation may well be one in which cities and their hinterlands, together, are understood as a basic political unit.

For America in general and for the West in particular, this way of thinking of the political role of cities, and of the political relationship of cities to their surrounding regions, would mark a significant change in political theory and practice. In the West, cities have always been viewed as a kind of incongruity, if not an embarrassment, in what we have thought of as a largely rural region. Politically, cities have been kept in a strictly subordinate position, closely hemmed in on all sides by state-mandated policy constraints. Whether the issue is taxation or subdivision control or nearly anything else beyond animal control ordinances, the power of local governments to determine their own policies and therby to shape their own futures has been severely limited by an incredibly detailed state code. In the West, this state paternalism toward local governments has been especially enhanced by the attitude of rural legislators, who have taken great care to insure that cities not acquire too much power over their own affairs. Against the background of the Jeffersonian attitude toward the relative political roles of cities and rural areas, this rural mistrust of cities is certainly understandable.

But as rural life is threatened more and more severely by international markets, by technological dislocations and corporate domination, it may be time for a reassessment of the relationship between cities and their rural environs. It may well be that neither towns nor farms can thrive in the way they would prefer until they turn their attention more directly to each other, realizing that they are mutually complementary parts of the enterprise of inhabiting a particular place—whether that place be called a bioregion, a city-state, or a *polis*. As a rule, we come closer to this way of thinking in the economic than in the political sphere. Cities and towns, in their economic development policies, recognize at least dimly that it is to their advantage to add value locally to the produce and raw materials of their hinterlands.

But by and large, these gropings in the direction of a more place-focused economy operate in a political setting to which cities and towns seem oblivious. Cities pursue their economic development strategies and rural areas pursue theirs with no recognition of how they might cooperate to strengthen one another's strategies. Such cooperation would require that city people and country people learn to listen to each other, build trust among each other, build patterns of working relationships which enable them to discover and build upon common ground. But this is a nation, and this is especially a region, where rural and city life have assumed so frequently an adversarial posture that the development of this kind of face-to-face, collaborative citizenship would be a major transformation. This is not the place to develop this suggestion in detail. But certainly, for the West in particular, the prospect for either its towns or its farms to prosper does not seem very bright without some new structures. The rediscovery of the politics of the *polis* may be an unsuspected part of the future of this old frontier.

Regardless of whether anything like city-states acquires some new elements of sovereignty, the effort to move beyond procedural deadlocks is likely to increase the pressure toward some form of decentralization. The old republican arguments are quite simply sound: any kind of active citizenship, where different interests are directly engaged in working out their problems and possibilities among themselves, is going to work better in small than in large political entities. The proceduralism of the federalist solution was an integral feature of the effort to create a single, powerful government "over so great an extent." Proceduralism and nationalism were born together and have grown together, and if the frontier of proceduralism is now showing signs of exhaustion, then we have to expect that the premise of national hegemony may also be called into question. Again, this is not the place to explore this possibility in detail, but at least one peculiarly Western aspect of it might shed some light on the larger topic of nationalism and decentralization.

In discussing how bureaucracy has come into the West side by side with rugged individualism, I referred earlier to the fact that large stretches of western land were reserved by the federal government when it granted statehood to places like Idaho, Montana, Wyoming, Utah, or New Mexico. Aside from Indian land and national parks, most of this land now falls under the jurisdiction of the Bureau of Land Management (in the case of grazing land), or, where the land is timbered, under the management of the Forest Service.

This pattern of federal ownership and management of Western land affects both the politics and the economics of the region. The concept of a place-focused economy—of a "marketplace"—is profoundly undermined by these extensive federal holdings. What emerges is neither a sense of inhabited *place* nor of a free *market*. National forest management illustrates this point. Both industry and environmentalists routinely berate the Forest Service for its anti-market activities. The wood products industry bemoans regulations and legislation which keep it from harvesting good, marketable timber, while environmentalists charge that many Forest Service timber sales have the effect of subsidizing the industry, especially by using public funds to build logging roads which an open market would not justify. Analogous arguments are levied against the Bureau of Land Management for its grazing land management. As both sides charge the federal bureaucracy with being the servant of the opposition, a potentially substantial arena of common ground is consistently ignored. In most cases, debate over federal policy centers on its effect on local economies. The question which everyone overlooks is whether federal control of resources makes the local economy weaker than any of the local contestants would choose.

In fact, federal control does have precisely that effect. This is due, very substantially, to the nature of federal bureaucratic decision making. Recall, once again, the Forest Service hearing on the proposed management plan for the Bridger-Teton National Forest. This decision making process is set up to encourage adversaries to make their respective cases to the neutral third party. We have already explored the consequences of this procedural approach for public discourse, and we have seen the consequences carried to their logical conclusion in the Dubois two-by-four debate. What is perhaps not so clear is that here the people of Dubois are dealing not only with a procedural politics, but also with a version of imperialism which encourages this kind of behavior. It is not simply that they are expected to present adversarial cases to a neutral third party, but to a "fed"—to a representative of a remote, powerful government which owns most of the land and resources upon which their livelihood and well-being depend.

It would be an insult to these people to assume that they are incapable of reaching some accommodation among themselves about how to inhabit their own place. Such accommodation would never be easy, and it would probably always be open to some redefinition. But if they were allowed to solve their problems (and manage their resources) themselves, they would soon discover that no one wants local sawmills closed, and no one wants wildlife habitat annihilated. If encouraged to collaborate, they would learn to inhabit the place on the place's own terms better than any regulatory bureaucracy will ever accomplish. But this kind of collaborative citizenship is withheld from them by a combination of proceduralism and imperialism.

At this point we have to speak of politics and economics in the same breath. If localities in the West had more control over their resources, and if the various interests within those localities could agree on some common directions for utilizing those resources, then local economies could be substantially strengthened and stabilized. But the political "ifs" which precede this economic "then" are significant indeed. This is plainly illustrated by the history of the Sagebrush Rebellion. In the early years of the Reagan presidency, as talk of the New Federalism gained currency and as the Reagan administration sought to sell off federal assets, a movement arose in the West to localize control of much of the region's federal land. After a few years of heated debate, the movement faded from the scene. As might have been expected, there was considerable nationalist opposition to this decentralist initiative, but in the end the politics of the West itself guaranteed the demise of the Sagebrush Rebellion.

The movement was led by conservatives, with particular support from grazing, timbering, and mining interests. Environmentalists and recreationists saw the rebellion (with considerable justification) as an effort to place public land in private hands, with one major objective: to increase the profit margins of various enterprises. In the end, an unusual opportunity for the West to gain some much-needed control over its own territory and resources was stalled by the distrust which so thoroughly characterizes western politics. It is on this level, finally, that the West must finally confront the challenge of cooperation which Stegner so tersely poses. The region cannot transcend its colonial heritage until it gains a much more substantial measure of indigenous control over its own land and resources. But it can neither gain nor exercise that control until the left and the right gain enough trust in each other, and establish a productive enough working relationship, to enable them to agree, at least roughly, on what they would seek to accomplish if they had such control. Certainly such agreement will not be easily achieved, but the time has come to turn and face each other and begin working toward it. Until that happens, the pattern of decision making about vast stretches of western land and vast stores of its resources will be simply a variation on the scene in Dubois. The end of those federally controlled debates is always a less satisfying way of inhabiting the place than any of the participants would have chosen. As more and more people become dissatisfied with this less-than-zero-sum solution of the procedural republic, it is time to look the alternative in the face. The alternative carries two inescapable implications: a challenge to nationally centralized control of western resources, and a new capacity for western adversaries to work out their own destiny among themselves.

This would be a tall enough order if those adversaries were all local, home-grown representatives of the right and the left. But the challenge is considerably heightened when we confront the fact that some of the major players on the stage are large corporations, often controlled by corporate executives and directors with no roots in the region at all. Does it really make sense to speak of an economics or a politics of inhabitation which depends upon the cooperation of those who are not genuine inhabitants?

This is not, of course, a new problem. Throughout American history, many of the most significant declines in the vitality of public life have been accompanied by a rise in the political influence of monied interests, and particularly of large corporations. To the extent that Jefferson was right in seeing the new Constitution as an overreaction to events like Shays' Rebellion, it was clearly the creditor class which was doing the reacting. Again in 1896, when republican principles under the populist banner surged to a new height of influence, it was Mark Hanna's brilliant orchestration of corporate money which stemmed the tide, resulting in what Lawrence Goodwyn characterizes as both a lasting decline in democratic self-confidence and a (so far) permanent entrenchment of corporate political power. Now, after another hundred years of political history, we witness a resurgence of interest in "republican principles," "civic virtue," and more "cooperative" approaches to political problem-solving. But many of those who worry about (and have often experienced) the effects of corporate political power are inclined to ask what is to be gained by trying to cooperate with multinational corporations. Talk of revitalizing public life by encouraging greater reliance upon civic virtue seems like the height of sentimentality, given the track record of many of these corporations. There is no easy or comprehensive answer to this problem. But unless we are willing to accept the accelerating pattern of blocked initiatives, we seem to have little choice but to look for answers that are neither easy nor comprehensive.

This problem of the role of corporations in public life helps to focus the larger problem of our declining capacity for being public at all. One of the reasons that corporations are a problem in public life is precisely because we have lost so much of our sense of public identity. Corporations have always existed at public dispensation. They have been allowed by the public to exist, in the peculiar form that they take, only because the public thought that it was going to get more than it would lose in the bargain. Corporations only become a problem in public life when the public loses its ability to enforce this bargain.

What the public was giving up used to be clearly understood. Primarily, it had to do with allowing a conglomeration of individuals to fashion themselves into a new kind of body, to assume a new "corporeal" existence, and in the process escape some of the inconveniences which attend upon being human. Mortality, for example, was something which humans had not well understood how to avoid before they learned to create corporations with a "perpetual" span of life. When individuals accumulated capital and then encountered the inconvenience of mortality, they had usually faced the further public inconvenience of inheritance taxes. Corporate stock, of course, was also subject to such taxes, but one of the fundamental purposes of a corporation is to allow certain pools of capital to be accumulated for reinvestment without having to distribute (or attribute) it to shareholders. That pool of accumulated wealth is thus freed from all the inconveniences of mortality. This is one of the ways in which the joining of individuals in the body of a corporation allows those individuals a broader scope of action than would otherwise be possible.

Another, even more crucial feature of corporations has always been the concept of limited liability. If I personally own a train and it runs over you, all of my personal assets are subject to your (or your heirs') claim for damages. But if I own stock in a corporate railroad which runs over you, only the corporation's assets are subject to your suit. My liability is limited to the stock I own; my personal assets are shielded. So on the one hand, corporations were intended to allow an unusual scope for accumulation of wealth within the corporation, while on the other hand they also were to shield the accumulation of wealth outside the corporation.

This is not to imply that there is anything wrong with any of this, or that the society should not have chosen to grant these and other special dispensations to corporations. The point is simply that this was in fact a public choice which was made and continues to be made not because corporations have any kind of inherent right to such treatment, but because it was thought that the public benefit would outweigh the public loss. In many ways it has, particularly where corporations have taken seriously their civic responsibilities. The problem is that corporations (armed with these publicly endowed tools for the accumulation of wealth) have grown so powerful in both the economic and political spheres that they are often able to dictate terms to the very public which allows them to exist in the first place. When this happens (and it does happen all too often), it marks a very substantial failure of our public life. A healthy public life would be one in which the public knows its own mind well enough and trusts its own will far enough that it would never allow itself to be controlled by its own creatures.

The last of the old frontier did not take long to learn about corporate influence in public life. Corporations had played a major role in most of the economic cycles of the region, even when it was the frontier. The penultimate life of the rugged individualist might be summed up in the mountain men who trapped beaver in the high headwaters of the Rocky Mountains. But even then "the Company" provided the supplies for the mountain men and accumulated the profits. This was to be the beginning of an unbroken chain—a pattern repeated time and again, and still a major factor in the economic life of the region. A resource is identified in the area—one for which a national or more often an international market is developing. Beaver, gold, silver, copper, oil, hydropower, coal, uranium—in each case, the pattern is the same: the region has no capital of its own to develop the resource, so the Company sends in the capital, develops the resource, and draws the profits back out of the region.

As the frontier closed up and the region was divided into states (each with a "republican form of government"), the relationship between corporate influence and the public interest was quickly drawn into focus. How will the Company be taxed? What environmental regulations will it be subjected to? How will it be required to treat its workers? From the earliest days of statehood the region experienced some of the most shocking and virulent forms of corporate domination of public life to be found anywhere in the nation. Time after time, on one issue after another, the fact that the area's economy depended so substantially upon outside sources of capital was brought home to the inhabitants as the threat was made and repeated: "If you do that, we'll shut this place down."

This has, of course, been only a part of the political history of the region, but it has been a substantial enough part to leave many people very leery of talk about "consensus politics" or "cooperation." To be sure, public interest groups have learned to cooperate among themselves, creating broad-based and often quite effective political coalitions aimed, among other things, at countering the worst manifestations of corporate political influence. But it is less and less clear how the public interest can be served without an effort to create political forms in which these groups are at least occasionally cooperating not only with each other but also with chambers of commerce, taxpayer associations, bankers, realtors—in general, "the other guys."

The alternative seems to be a deepening entanglement with the politics of "anybody wrecking anything." That brand of politics is as devastating to the public interest as it is to free enterprise. Every time a citizen group or a business, a city council or a state legislature finds itself stalemated by the mutual blocking of initiative, a few more citizens conclude that the political system just doesn't work. From then on, if they enter the public realm at all, it will be only to protect their own private interests. They are no longer citizens; they are now just taxpayers, and as such they will be at best neutral, at worst adversarial to public interest causes. Very few of these people will be brought back into politics by democratic appeals to the public interest, but many of them might be mobilized by more regressive or authoritarian appeals. The lesson can hardly be overstated: proponents of the public interest must find ways to break out of the politics of stalemate, even if it means (as it does) that they have to begin opening up arenas of cooperation with "the enemy."

But the other side is learning much the same lesson. One of the great strengths of modern business enterprises has been their capacity to plan effectively, to project their activities accurately into the future. In a setting of escalating deadlock, however, this cherished corporate strength is less and less reliable. In addition, there are direct costs of confrontation which any wise corporation would minimize if it could. Hearings, lawsuits, and appeals cost money; they represent a serious drain on corporate productivity. For the corporation as much as for its "public interest" adversaries, then, cooperation offers some advantages, provided always that the costs are not too high.

Any effort to heighten the capacity of these two camps for cooperation will quickly bring into focus the old republican notion of "civic virtue." It is simply impossible for people with widely divergent interests to work effectively together unless they develop some patterns of relationship which finally resolve themselves into precisely those virtues. Remember the story of the pulp mill and the environmental group: the one indispensable element of that collaboration was the establishment of a pattern of mutual trust between the two parties. Behind trust lie virtues like honesty and fairness. Nothing will substitute for those virtues; nothing else will get the job done.

What this implies is that such cooperation or collaboration is in fact an exercise in citizenship, in the classic sense of that word. Citizens are people possessed of civic virtues who relate to each other, solve problems, realize possibilities by the exercise of those virtues. But this, in turn, implies that corporations must be capable of citizenship on a local level. This must be more than a public-relations variety of citizenship; it must be the kind of citizenship that is real enough to inspire trust. Above all, such citizenship must demonstrate a genuine and reliable responsiveness to the place, a full-fledged participation in the human project of living well in that place. If the place is defined and nurtured by a river, then the corporation must make the care of the river one of its priorities; it must contribute its fair share toward that project. If inhabitation of the place depends upon the sustained production of timber, the corporation must either take on the task of nurturing forests or else forego its claim to citizenship. If inhabitation means looking beyond the extraction of a nonrenewable resource to the building of a replacement economy once the mine closes, then the mining corporation, if it is going to call itself (and claim the advantages of being) a corporate citizen, must put its shoulder to the wheel (through severance taxes or some genuine alternative) to help build that replacement economy.

Left to themselves, of course, corporations are not going to practice citizenship in this way. The main reason is that they are not inhabitants in the same way that other residents of the place are. Once the mine plays out or the large sawlogs are all cut, the corporation can simply leave—a pattern all too familiar in the West. The corporation's chief loyalty is not to the place, but to the shareholders and executives who almost always live somewhere else. A realistic appraisal of the situation will take account of this semiinhabitory feature of the corporation. But having taken this factor into consideration, the politics of inhabitation need not be stopped cold in its tracks. Here, the "art of the possible" must turn from the half-empty glass to the one that is half full. The politics of inhabitation must realize its own possibilities, in part by nurturing citizenship among its corporations.

Nurturing here implies a proper understanding of relationship—a relationship rather like that of a family, where the community—the republic—understands once again not only that it is prior to the corporation, but also that it can and should create the environment and set the limits within which these, its creatures, are to be nurtured, developed, and allowed to thrive. What this means, among other things, is that the terms of corporate citizenship are clearly understood not to be wholly voluntary. Just as parents have a responsibility to set rules for participation in a household, so the republic should be calmly comfortable with its responsibility to define and enforce the basic ground rules for inhabitation of any particular jurisdiction.

This may seem too elementary to be worth saying, but somehow we have lost sight of this fundamental relationship. In doing so, we have harmed both sides of the relationship. All too often, the body politic acts like a parent who is intimidated by its own children, too uncertain of its own role to perform it with any consistency. The result, of course, is inconsistency—an often maddening vacillation between permissiveness and arbitrary displays of authority. While corporations might prefer a straight regimen of permissiveness, most of them realize that this is a dream beyond attainment. Within the real world, business enterprises consistently argue that they are willing to subject themselves to reasonable rules and guidelines, provided there is some consistency in their application. In a sense, corporations seem to understand better than their public "parent" the appropriate relationship between them. Corporations understand that they are derivative, that they must live within prescribed constraints. They have no profound objection to that reality, but they often find themselves living in the household of a parent who is unable to provide an environment which is at once stable and nurturing.

Like most relationship problems, this one can probably only be solved by a mutual pattern of change and development affecting both parties. For example, a corporation which learns to practice genuine citizenship creates, by that very development, a marginally more effective body politic. How does that happen? In the case of the pulp mill's wastewater discharge permit, the corporation (as well as its environmental adversary) transformed the decision making process simply by assuming the mantle of citizenship. Instead of appearing as adversaries before a neutral third-party decision maker, they in effect chose to make the decision themselves by solving the discharge problem collaboratively. This shouldering of responsibility releases the state agency from its accustomed role of having to choose between permissiveness and authoritarianism. In that prevailing model, whichever way the state chooses to go, it is immediately subject to a campaign from the losing party to reverse its decision, in this or in future cases. But when the adversaries become the decision makers, there is less likely to be a losing side; instead, both parties acquire a stake in the stability of the chosen solution.

This kind of citizenship recaptures the very essence of democracy; it makes government far less a matter of bureaucracy, far more a matter of the direct exercise of citizen competence. But as people (and corporations) experience what it is to be the government, that government itself gains legitimacy and strength. It is the mutually distrusted third-party decision maker (on the model of the Forest Service) which resembles a parent uncertain of its relationship to its children. But this is not simply "the government's" problem, nor can the government solve it by itself. The solution must be sought on the level of citizenship. A healthy, calmly self-confident government can only be developed by turning adversary factions and interests into problem-solving citizens.

We can at least begin to imagine, then, how a more place-centered version of corporate citizenship might emerge as a facet of the renewal of the larger civic culture. The process would begin with a hardheaded assessment of self-interest. Taking account of factors like the costs of confrontation and the endless uncertainties of adversarial decision making, a few corporations in a given locale might begin to experiment, as the pulp mill did, with a collaborative approach to problem-solving. (The local managers are likely to encounter skepticism from the head office when this is first suggested. Missoula's pulp mill manager chuckles when he recalls his corporate superiors saying, "You want to do *what?*" when he told them he wanted to negotiate a solution with his environmental adversaries.)

If the collaboration produces good results, the corporation is likely to become an advocate for a more widespread use of such an approach. There are at least two reasons for this. One is simply the power of good ideas; they are worth sharing. The other is more subtle and brings us back again to the reality of political life. By choosing collaboration, this corporation has decided to minimize the risks and the costs of the either/or adversarial model. This choice involves giving up the chance to win big by persuading the third-party decision maker to opt for the most permissive alternative. The corporation which chooses the path of collaborative problem-solving has probably decided that, in the long run, there is more to be gained by foregoing the erratic occurrence of the big win. But having made that decision, the corporation acquires a stake in narrowing the availability of the permissive option to other actors, including at the very least its own competitors. It is as if, by choosing citizenship as against the option of the "unencumbered self," one automatically wills that one's neighbors also choose citizenship. Otherwise, they are likely to become "free riders," taking unfair advantage of the concessions which others have made in the interest of the common good.

There is some reason to hope, then, that the development of a deeper practice of corporate citizenship could prove to be a cumulative process. Part of that process is the gradual strengthening of the republic, but it is important to note that what becomes stronger is not the bureaucracy, but democracy itself. In this process the state would acquire an enhanced ability to enforce the rules and limits which inhabitation implies, yet by and large those limits would become both more predictable and less coercive (more self-imposed) than they currently are.

I do not mean to minimize the factors that stand in the way of a genuinely inhabitory kind of citizenship on the part of corporations, particularly those extractive industries which depend, to a certain extent, upon the West remaining a colony for the rest of the nation. The hurdles are very substantial and very deeply rooted. But it is a mistake to assume that all of those problems derive from the nature of the corporation itself, and that they are therefore beyond public control. A large part of the corporate problem in public life is the public's problem, stemming from its own lack of a clear identity. That lack of identity, in turn, stems from our overall failure to demand of ourselves an active practice of citizenship. Until corporations are presented with a public which understands and practices citizenship, their own capacity for citizenship will never be fully brought into play. What is the extent or what are the limits of their civic capacity? The answer is simply not knowable in advance. Citizenship is one of those practices which defines its field of operation as it evolves. MacIntyre describes this developmental nature of all genuine practices:

> What is distinctive in a practice is in part the way in which conceptions of the relevant goods and ends which the technical skills serve . . . are transformed and enriched by these extensions of human powers and by that regard for its own internal goods which are partially definitive of each particular practice or type of practice. Practices never have a goal or goals fixed for all time—painting has no such goal nor has physics—but the goals themselves are transmuted by the history of the activity.[12]

If citizenship were to become a practice, then it too would shape its own possibilities as it developed. This would apply to the possibility of corporate citizenship and to the broader possibility of a politics of inhabitation. In chapter 4, I asked what might be the future of public life in the area which became the last of the old American frontier. If we cannot turn the clock back to some imagined golden age, if we choose not to hurtle into a future which destroys most of what makes life worth living in the region, and if our current politics of polarization is steadily undermining both our public life and our capacity to shape a viable economy, then we need to try to envision a fourth way. We can now make some educated guesses about a few possible components of that fourth alternative—an alternative which I have spoken of as the "politics of inhabitation."

This is a politics which synthesizes realism and hope, blending them in the crucible which inhabiting hard country provides. Wendell Berry speaks of the project of living well in hard country, in terms which describe fairly precisely this fundamental paradox of the politics of inhabitation. In his poem, "Work Song," Berry writes:

> This is no paradisal dream.
> Its hardship is its opportunity.[13]

A politics which finds its opportunity in its hardship, in its limitations, and more particularly in the limitations of its place, is a politics which captures the dual meaning of politics as the "art of the possible" and at the same time recaptures the ancient meaning of politics as the project of inhabiting a *polis*.

Such a politics would be a change from what we now know, in many ways. It will depend less upon procedures and bureacracies and more upon human virtues and patterns of relationship. It will be a much less centralized politics; the national presence will be substantially diminished. In the West, this would imply that the people who live here would claim a much larger share of dominion over their own territory. Yet this can only happen when the people of the West learn to listen to each other and to work effectively on the project of inhabitation. Cooperation is central to the politics of inhabitation, and it will have to extend to cooperation between right and left, between Democrats and Republicans, even between environmentalists and corporations. Finally, this politics will not come into its own until cities and their rural surroundings learn to appreciate the common stake they have in one another's welfare. The new politics in the West will be successful only if it is willing to carry decentralization even further than states' rights—back to the *polis* itself. In the rediscovery of the city-state as the locus of inhabitation, politics might be renewed.

But it is also in the rediscovery of the city-state that America's ambivalence about the relationship of cities and their rural surroundings might begin to be resolved. In chapter 2 we encountered Jefferson's doomed hope that agriculture would always have new frontiers to expand into so that farming, and with it civic virtue, would maintain a predominant place in American life. Meanwhile, Hegel argued that America would not become civilized—would not become a civil society—until it exhausted the frontier so that people began facing each other in cities. This question of where civic life really resides—in the city or in the country—has remained alive for over two centuries. What the concept of inhabitation may teach us is that the dichotomy is a misleading one—that real politics resides exactly in that unique blending of city and country which, as the *polis* or city-state, is fundamental to politics.

Hegel had argued that America would not develop a genuine public dimension until it stopped escaping from itself and turned (especially through the maturing of its cities) to face itself. For this region, that turning has always had a special significance. We usually think of the pattern of American settlement in terms of westward expansion. But the last regions settled within the Lower Forty-eight were not, in fact, the most westerly. When Frederick Jackson Turner finally declared the frontier closed a century ago, it was not because the Pacific shore had been reached and settled—that had happened long since—but because the high, dry, lonely stretches of the Northern Rockies and the adjoining plains had been filled in enough that they were no longer frontier. No small part of that settlement was done by people who had in fact gone on to the coast (especially to Oregon) and then, finding not quite the frontier they had been seeking, had turned back eastward again, recrossed the mountains, and cast their lot finally with country which was still "open" for one reason alone: because it (and the people who were already inhabiting it) so fiercely resisted white settlement. Dick Summers, having guided settlers to Oregon in A. B. Guthrie's *The Way West*, turns back toward the headwaters at the outset of *Fair Land, Fair Land*, driven eastward now to find the open country that had drawn so many west.

> Dick Summers climbed the ridge from the channeled valley, glad enough to be leaving Oregon behind him. He hadn't said goodbye to any of the wagon-train people who had hired him for a guide. Goodbyes were something like gravestones. Yeah, rest in peace, you sodbusters. May the Lord bless you, good men and weak. . . . Here's hoping your plows pay off in berries or in melons or apples or whatever. . . .
>
> Even high on the ridge the breath of the Pacific reached him, wet enough and salt enough to pickle pork in. Going east he was, going east to find the west, the west of wind and open skies and buffalo. Hurrah for that. . . .
>
> He squirmed back from the cliff's edge and started walking again. Here had been beaver country all right, but give him the Popo Agie and the Wind and the Seeds-kee-dee and throw in the upper Missouri in spite of the Blackfeet. Give him a far reach of the eye, the grasses rippling, the small streams talking, buttes swimming clear a hundred miles away. Give him not Mount Hood, but the clean, ungodly upthrust of the Tetons. They were some.[14]

"Going east to find the west"—that is more than a small part of the story of the headwaters. Passed over in the great drive to the Pacific, passed over for being too cold, too hot, too dry, too far from any market or any reasonable access to market, the region remained wilderness longer than places east and west and attracted only those who could love a wilderness. Later, of course, the metal seekers came, and finally the sodbusters who had no other place to homestead any more. But for a long time the remoteness and the harshness of the land kept people at arm's length, and even now not a few of those who do come into the country come for reasons not totally unlike those that brought Dick Summers. Yet at the same time the country has always made cooperation a condition of its inhabitation.

This, then, is the region in which Americans finally began the slow process of "turning back upon themselves"—where they finally had to begin going East to find the West. In that sense, this region's story is a vital part of the larger American story. Robert Frost seems to allude to this theme in a poem entitled "West-Running Brook":

> Speaking of contraries, see how the brook
> In that white wave runs counter to itself.
> It is from that in water we were from
> Long, long before we were from any creature. . . .
>
> It is this backward motion toward the source,
> Against the stream, that most we see ourselves in,
> The tribute of the current to the source.
> It is from this in nature we are from.
> It is most us.[15]

It was another American poet, T. S. Eliot, who drove himself even further back to the source. From England, Eliot wrote four place-focused poems—the Four Quartets. In "Little Gidding" he described what may yet be the story of American public life, and especially of public life here at the last of the American frontier:

> We shall not cease from exploration
> And the end of all our exploring
> Will be to arrive where we started
> And know the place for the first time.[16]

Notes

1. George Bernard Shaw, *Back to Methuselah*, Pt. I, Act I.
2. *Great Falls Tribune*, June 29, 1983, p. 2.
3. Frederick Jackson Turner, *The Significance of the Frontier in American History*, p. 223.
4. Lawrence Goodwyn, *The Populist Moment*, p. 265.
5. Paulo Freire, *Pedagogy of the Oppressed*, p. 80.
6. Robert B. Reich, *The Next American Frontier*.
7. Wallace Stegner, *The Sound of Mountain Water*, pp. 37–38.
8. George F. Will, *Statecraft as Soulcraft*, pp. 163–64.
9. Benjamin Barber, *Strong Democracy*, pp. 200, 201.
10. Michael Ignatieff, *The Needs of Strangers*, p. 107.
11. This presents us with another sense in which it may be said that the American frontier was a denial of politics. In this case, the white invaders did not consider the price of removing the native inhabitants to be too high. There can be no politics of inhabitation under those terms.
12. Alasdair MacIntyre, *After Virtue*, pp. 193–94.
13. Wendell Berry, "Work Song," in *Clearing*, p. 32.
14. A. B. Guthrie, *Fair Land, Fair Land*, pp. 3–4.
15. Robert Frost, "West-Running Brook," in *Selected Poems of Robert Frost*, p. 165.
16. T. S. Eliot, "Little Gidding," in *The Complete Poems and Plays, 1909–1950*, p. 145.

Bibliography

Books

Arendt, Hannah. *The Human Condition*. Chicago: The University of Chicago Press, 1958.

Axelrod, Robert. *The Evolution of Cooperation*. New York: Basic Books, 1984.

Barber, Benjamin. *Strong Democracy*. Berkeley: University of California Press, 1984.

Bellah, Robert N., et al. *Habits of the Heart*. Berkeley: University of California Press, 1985.

Berry, Wendell. *Clearing*. New York: Harcourt Brace Jovanovich, 1977.

———. *The Unsettling of America*. New York: Avon Books, 1977.

Borgmann, Albert. *Technology and the Character of Contemporary Life*. Chicago: the University of Chicago Press, 1984.

Boyte, Harry C. *Community is Possible*. New York: Harper & Row, 1984.

Eliot, T. S. *The Complete Poems and Plays, 1909–1950*. New York: Harcourt, Brace & World, 1971.

Freire, Paulo. *Pedagogy of the Oppressed*. New York: Continuum, 1984.

Frost, Robert. *Selected Poems of Robert Frost*. New York: Holt, Rinehart and Winston, 1966.

Garreau, Joel. *The Nine Nations of North America*. Boston: Houghton Mifflin, 1981.

Gilligan, Carol. *In a Different Voice: Psychological Theory and Women's Development*. Cambridge: Harvard University Press, 1982.

Goodwyn, Lawrence. *The Populist Moment*. New York: Oxford University Press, 1978.

Guthrie, A. B. *Fair Land, Fair Land*. Boston: Houghton-Mifflin Co., 1982.

Hamilton, Alexander; James Madison; and John Jay. *The Federalist Papers*. New York: New American Library, 1961.

Haworth, Lawrence. *The Good City*. Bloomington: Indiana University Press, 1963.

Hegel, Georg Wilhelm Friedrich. *The Philosophy of History*. Trans. J. Sibree. New York: Willey Book Co., 1944.

Ignatieff, Michael. *The Needs of Strangers*. New York: Penguin Books, 1984.

Jacobs, Jane. *Cities and the Wealth of Nations*. New York: Vintage Books, 1984.

Jeffers, Robinson. *The Selected Poetry of Robinson Jeffers*. New York: Random House, 1937.

Jefferson, Thomas. *Notes on the State of Virginia*. New York: Harper & Row, 1964.

————. *The Papers of Thomas Jefferson*. Ed. Julian P. Boyd. Princeton: Princeton University Press, 1952.

MacIntyre, Alasdair. *After Virtue*. Notre Dame, Indiana: University of Notre Dame Press, 1984.

Madison, James. *Notes of Debates in the Federal Convention of 1787*. Athens: Ohio University Press, 1966.

McPhee, John. *Coming into the Country*. New York: Farrar, Straus and Giroux, 1977.

Montesquieu, Charles, Baron de. *The Spirit of Laws*. Trans. Thomas Nugent. London: George Bell & Sons, 1906.

Poston, Richard. *Small Town Renaissance: A Story of the Montana Study*. New York: Harper & Brothers, 1950.

Reich, Robert B. *The Next American Frontier*. New York: Penguin Books, 1987.

Sale, Kirkpatrick. *Dwellers in the Land: The Bioregional Vision*. San Francisco: Sierra Club Books, 1985.

Shaw, George Bernard. *Back to Methuselah*. New York: Brentano's, 1921.

Stegner, Wallace. *The Sound of Mountain Water*. New York: Doubleday & Company, 1969.

Sullivan, William M. *Reconstructing Public Philosophy*. Berkeley: University of California Press, 1982.

Susskind, Lawrence, and Jeffrey Cruikshank. *Breaking the Impasse: Consensual Approaches to Resolving Public Disputes*. New York: Basic Books, 1987.

Thurow, Lester C. *The Zero-Sum Society*. New York: Penguin Books, 1980.

Toole, K. Ross. *Montana: An Uncommon Land*. Norman: University of Oklahoma Press, 1959.

————. *Rape of the Great Plains*. Boston: Little, Brown, 1976.

————. *Twentieth Century Montana: A State of Extremes*. Norman: University of Oklahoma Press, 1972.

Turner, Frederick Jackson. *The Frontier in American History*. Washington, D.C.: Government Printing Office, 1894.

Unger, Roberto Mangabeira. *Knowledge and Politics*. New York: The Free Press, 1984.

Will, George F. *Statecraft as Soulcraft*. New York: Simon & Schuster, 1983.

Articles

Ford, Pat. "Idaho Watershed." *Northern Lights Magazine* 2, no. 5:18–19.

Janklow, William. "High Noon in the Missouri River Basin." In *Boundaries Carved in Water*. The Missouri River Brief Series, No. 4. Missoula: Northern Lights Institute, 1988.

Sandel, Michael J. "Morality and the Liberal Ideal." *New Republic*, May, 1984, p. 16.

————. "The Procedural Republic and the Unencumbered Self." *Political Theory* 12 (February, 1984):81–96.

Winthrop, John. "A Modell of Christian Charity," written on board the Arbella, on the Atlantic Ocean, 1630. In *Collections of the Massachusetts Historical Society*, Vol. 27. Boston: Charles C. Little and James Brown, 1838.

Unpublished Speeches

Gardner, John. Speech delivered to the Humphrey Institute, April 3, 1980.

Snyder, Gary. Remarks given at the "Reinhabitation Conference" at North San Juan School, held under the auspices of the California Council on the Humanities, August, 1976.

Index